WILLIAMS-SONOMA

NEW FLAVORS FOR
chicken

RECIPES
Rick Rodgers

PHOTOGRAPHS
Tucker + Hossler

Oxmoor
House ®

spring

summer

fall

winter

introducing new flavors

To get a chicken dish on the table—a roasted bird, sautéed breasts, grilled parts— even an accomplished cook depends on a repertory of basic techniques. But how do you keep these familiar cooking methods from turning into predictable dinners? The answer is to reinvigorate classic dishes with fresh, high-impact ingredients and add tasty elements of surprise. These new flavors come from places both near and far: locally grown, farm-fresh produce and the bold seasonings of global cuisines.

Fruits, vegetables, and herbs at the height of their seasons are also at the pinnacle of flavor. Take the time to seek out the best produce at local farmstands and farmers' markets—you'll be giving yourself a flavorful base to work from and a head start on creating a wonderful dish. Carefully grown, freshly harvested ingredients can elevate even the simplest recipe to a dish of distinction.

Seasonings from the far reaches of the world that were once considered exotic can now be found on many supermarket shelves, and, with very little effort, they can add lively accents to your cooking. Invite these ingredients into your kitchen and let them inspire combinations that intrigue the palate. Pairing these international elements with the finest fresh produce creates bold, amplified flavor.

The forty-four recipes in this book will seem familiar, but will taste new: They are all modern twists on poultry classics. Organized by season, the recipes encourage you to cook with the season's ripe bounty and take advantage of what's fresh and flavorful. With light dishes in spring and summer, and rich, hearty ones in fall and winter, the recipes are tailored to deliciously sate your seasonal cravings.

freshness as an ingredient

Freshness is the single most important element that makes a dish a stand out. From the bird to the herbs, purchase the freshest, highest-quality ingredients you can find. They form the foundation for every delectable chicken dish in this book.

seasonal These days, many types of produce at the supermarket are flown in from all over the world, making them, in effect, season-less. But the best, ripest flavors are found in the fruits and vegetables that are in season in your area. So, while it is possible to buy peaches and tomatoes in January, it's really the root vegetables and winter squashes that are the most flavorful. Think in terms of the seasonal cycles and turn to the local bounty for culinary inspiration.

local Pay a visit to a local farmstand or farmers' market for the freshest, best-quality fruits and vegetables. Instead of spending time traveling to get to market, produce that is grown nearby can stay on the tree or in the ground longer where it develops just a little more goodness, so you're assured both freshness and flavor. For poultry, buy from a local butcher who is an expert on quality chicken, turkey, and duck. Buying locally has an added benefit: You are supporting businesses in the community.

organic To find fruits and vegetables of the very highest quality, it often means selecting organic produce. Organically grown fruits, vegetables, and herbs have not been treated with synthetic pesticides or preservatives, and the care that went into farming them can be tasted. The same is true for poultry. A couple dollars more for minimally processed chicken—the main ingredient in all of these recipes—is money well spent. (Turn to page 142 for more information on different types of chicken.)

being bold

Chicken is a versatile ingredient with a mild taste, making it a blank canvas for a colorful palette of flavors. The recipes in this book are not restrained in their approach—they showcase assertive flavors from all over the world.

global seasonings From Argentina to Vietnam, the inspiration for many of these recipes comes from places across the globe. Luckily for us, ingredients once considered exotic are now easy to find: Indian curry powder and Thai curry paste, Sriracha sauce and North African harissa, Spanish smoked paprika and Chinese five-spice all share space on supermarket shelves. They offer quick ways to add big bursts of flavor; one taste and they may quickly become your new culinary allies.

high-impact flavors Not all bold flavors come from far away sources. Tart cranberries, peppery arugula, orange marmalade, and green olives are all familiar ingredients that offer big taste and instantly add character to chicken dishes. High-impact ingredients often require elements to balance their assertiveness—for example, cranberries need a sweetener—but along with the balance always comes depth and complexity, and richly satisfying flavors.

flavorful cooking methods Cooking techniques that coax the most flavor from your ingredients add distinction to your recipes. Whole spices benefit from being toasted and freshly ground. Brining chicken, or soaking it in a seasoned liquid, adds flavor that penetrates deep into the meat. Using browned pan drippings in a simple pan sauce adds a remarkably rich meatiness. Scattering soaked wood chips over glowing coals infuses a chicken with irresistible smokiness as it grills.

flavors in layers

A dish with full, round flavor simply tastes good. Sweet, sour, hot, and salty are the basic building blocks for taste—when thoughtfully layered into a recipe, they bring delicious depth and complexity even to the simplest preparations. The same is true of texture, an element that is sometimes overlooked. When a dish is both texturally balanced and full-flavored, it is wholly satisfying.

taste Sometimes a recipe calls for complementary tastes, in the way that woodsy thyme completes the earthiness of mushrooms. Other times, it calls for contrasting ones, as when the saltiness of miso is countered by the sweetness of sugar. An accent, such as heat from black pepper or fresh ginger, adds yet another dimension. Layered flavors create dishes that will pique your interest from the first taste and engage your palate until the very last bite.

texture Texture plays a surprisingly important role in the appeal of a dish. A one-note texture quickly becomes dull, but when each bite is slightly different from the last or when the recipe includes a range of pleasing textural components, the dish is captivating from start to finish. For example, a crisp crust makes fried chicken irresistible; chunky root vegetables add hearty substance to a braised chicken dish; tortilla chips sprinkled over lime soup add a welcome crunch.

Drawing spirit and taste from bountiful in-season fruits and vegetables and from a world of bold seasonings, the recipes that follow are deliciously fresh perspectives on familiar dishes. They will help get exciting, flavor-intense chicken dinners on the table, and, at the same time, inspire you to add new flavors to all of your cooking.

spring

sautéed chicken breasts with fava beans and green garlic

kosher salt and freshly ground pepper

fava beans in their pods, 2 pounds, shelled

green garlic, 2

boneless, skinless chicken breast halves, 4 (about 6 ounces each)

extra-virgin olive oil, 2 tablespoons

unsalted butter, 2 tablespoons

dry white wine or vermouth, ¼ cup

low-sodium chicken broth or stock, ¾ cup

MAKES 4 SERVINGS

Bring a saucepan of lightly salted water to a boil over high heat. Add the fava beans and cook just until the outer skins loosen, about 2 minutes. Drain well and rinse under cold running water until cool. Pinch each bean to remove its tough outer skin. You should end up with about ¾ cup beans. Coarsely chop the white and pale green bottoms of the green garlic and set aside. Thinly slice the green tops and set aside separately.

Preheat the oven to 200°F. Using a flat meat pounder, pound each chicken breast half until flattened to an even thickness of about ¾ inch. Season the chicken breasts with 1 teaspoon salt and ½ teaspoon pepper.

In a large frying pan, heat the oil over medium-high heat until very hot but not smoking. Add the chicken breasts and cook, without disturbing, until golden brown, 3–4 minutes. Turn and cook until the second sides are golden and the chicken springs back when pressed in the center, about 4 minutes. Transfer to a rimmed baking sheet and keep warm in the oven.

Pour off the fat from the frying pan. Return the pan to medium-high heat, add 1 tablespoon of the butter, and allow it to melt. Add the green garlic bottoms and sauté until wilted, about 1 minute, then add the wine and cook, scraping up the browned bits from the pan bottom, until almost evaporated, about 30 seconds. Add the fava beans and ¼ cup of the broth, cover, and cook, stirring occasionally, until tender, about 3 minutes. Stir in the remaining ½ cup broth and bring to a boil. Remove from the heat and stir in the remaining 1 tablespoon butter. Taste and adjust the seasonings.

Transfer the chicken to a carving board. Cut each breast half across the grain into slices about ½ inch thick and transfer to warmed dinner plates. Spoon some of the fava beans and sauce over each breast. Sprinkle with the green garlic tops and serve right away.

Green garlic resembles stocky green onions. It imparts a sweet, mild garlic flavor, without much garlicky heat, so you can use the fragrant stalks with abandon. In this recipe, green garlic complements the earthy, pleasing bitterness of fresh fava beans to create a chicken dish that is a tribute to spring.

baked chicken with vidalia onion sauce

Sweet onions are markedly more mellow and sugary than typical cooking onions. Here, Georgia's Vidalia onions are roasted to intensify their natural sugars and then combined with sherry, which contributes a distinctive nuttiness to the sauce.

Preheat the oven to 425°F. Lightly oil a large flameproof roasting pan.

Brush the skin of the chicken breast halves with 1 tablespoon of the oil. Season the breasts with 2 teaspoons salt and ½ teaspoon pepper, then sprinkle with the minced rosemary. Place the chicken, skin side up, in the center of the prepared pan. Place the onions in a bowl. Drizzle with the remaining 1 tablespoon oil and toss to coat evenly. Season the onions with ½ teaspoon each salt and pepper and toss again. Place the onions around the edges of the roasting pan.

Roast, stirring the onions occasionally, until the chicken is golden brown and an instant-read thermometer inserted in the thickest part of the breast meat registers 170°F, about 35 minutes. Transfer the chicken to a serving platter and tent with aluminum foil to keep warm. Raise the oven temperature to 475°F, and continue roasting the onions until they are very tender and deep beige, about 5 minutes longer.

Transfer the onions and any pan juices to a food processor. Place the roasting pan over medium-high heat. Add the sherry and broth and bring to a boil, scraping up the browned bits from the pan bottom. Boil until the liquid is reduced to ¾ cup, about 2 minutes. Remove from the heat.

Process the onions, adding as much of the liquid from the roasting pan as needed to make a pourable sauce. Taste and adjust the seasonings. Pour some of the sauce over the chicken, garnish with the rosemary sprigs, and serve right away. Pass the remaining sauce at the table.

extra-virgin olive oil, 2 tablespoons, plus oil for the roasting pan

bone-in, skin-on chicken breast halves, 4 (about ¾ pound each)

kosher salt and freshly ground pepper

fresh rosemary, 1 tablespoon minced, plus sprigs for garnish

vidalia onions, 2 large (1½ pounds total weight), cut into quarters

dry sherry, ¼ cup

low-sodium chicken broth or stock, ¾ cup

MAKES 4 SERVINGS

The arrival of baby vegetables in farmers' markets signals the start of spring. Subtly flavored, they're best used in light dishes and seasoned simply. A clear soup infused with citrusy lemongrass is the perfect showcase.

lemongrass-chicken soup with baby spring vegetables

Lemongrass lends its heady citrus fragrance and gentle herbal hints to this vegetable-rich soup with a Southeast Asian flavor profile. The fresh, clean taste it imparts is made fuller and more complex by the sweet pepperiness of ginger and the welcome heat of spicy Thai chiles.

Peel the dry outer layers of the lemongrass stalk to reveal the tender interior. Using a chef's knife, cut off the top of the stalk where it begins to toughen and discard it. Cut the bottom of the stalk in half crosswise. Peel the ginger, then cut it crosswise into 2 or 3 rounds. Crush the lemongrass and ginger with the flat side of the knife. Slice the chile into very thin rounds, leaving the seeds intact.

In a large saucepan over high heat, combine the lemongrass, ginger, half of the chile slices, the broth, soy sauce, shallot, and garlic, and bring to a simmer. Reduce the heat to low, cover, and simmer for 20 minutes.

Meanwhile, season the chicken breast halves with ½ teaspoon salt and ¼ teaspoon pepper. When the broth has simmered for 20 minutes, add the chicken, raise the heat to medium-low, cover, and cook at a brisk simmer until the chicken shows no sign of pink when pierced with the tip of a sharp knife near the bone, about 30 minutes. Transfer the chicken to a large plate to cool slightly, keeping the broth covered and at a simmer. Remove and discard the skin and bones, then shred the chicken into bite-sized pieces.

Remove and discard the lemongrass and ginger from the broth. Add the zucchini, yellow and pattypan squashes, carrots, and shredded chicken to the pan, cover, and continue to simmer until the vegetables are just tender, about 5 minutes. Taste the broth and adjust the seasonings.

Divide the soup evenly among warmed bowls and garnish with cilantro sprigs. Serve right away. Pass the remaining chile slices, cilantro, and lime wedges at the table.

lemongrass, 1 stalk

fresh ginger, one ½-inch piece

thai or serrano chile, 1

low-sodium chicken broth or stock, 4 cups

soy sauce, 2 tablespoons

shallot, 1, minced

garlic, 2 cloves, minced

bone-in, skin-on chicken breast halves, 4 (about 10 ounces each)

kosher salt and freshly ground pepper

baby zucchini, 6, cut in half on the diagonal

baby yellow squash, 6, cut in half lengthwise

baby pattypan squash, 6, cut in half pole to pole

baby carrots, 6, cut in half lengthwise

fresh cilantro sprigs for garnish

lime, 1, cut into 8 wedges

MAKES 4 SERVINGS

parchment-baked chicken with new potatoes, peas, and tarragon

boneless, skinless chicken breast halves, 4 (about 6 ounces each)

kosher salt and freshly ground pepper

unsalted butter, 4 tablespoons, at room temperature

dijon mustard, 2 teaspoons

fresh tarragon, 2 teaspoons minced

shallot, 1 teaspoon minced

new potatoes, 4, cut into ¼-inch rounds

english peas in their pods, ¾ pound, shelled

dry white wine, 4 tablespoons

MAKES 4 SERVINGS

Using a flat meat pounder, pound each chicken breast half until flattened to an even thickness of about ½ inch. Season the chicken breasts with 1 teaspoon salt and ½ teaspoon pepper. In a small bowl, mix together the butter, mustard, tarragon, and shallot. Season to taste with salt and pepper.

Preheat the oven to 400°F. Bring a saucepan of lightly salted water to a boil over high heat. Add the potatoes and cook for 2 minutes. Add the peas, cook for 2 minutes longer, and then drain the vegetables well.

Cut four 12-by-15-inch rectangles of parchment paper. Lay 1 piece, with a long side facing you, on a work surface. Fold it in half crosswise. Crease about 1 inch on the three open sides of the fold. Using scissors, and cutting on the diagonal, trim off about 2 inches from the two open corners. Unfold the parchment and center a chicken breast half on one side of the center fold. Layer the ingredients on top of the chicken: one-fourth of the butter mixture, one-fourth of the potato slices, one-fourth of the peas, and 1 tablespoon of the wine. Season lightly with salt and pepper.

Fold the paper back over the chicken, matching the edges. Starting at one end of the fold, fold the edges toward the chicken, making a series of small, tight folds to create a curved border around the chicken. Twist the end of the packet to create a tight seal. Transfer the packet to a rimmed baking sheet. Repeat with the remaining ingredients and parchment rectangles.

Bake until the paper packets puff up, about 20 minutes. To test for doneness, press the chicken with a fingertip through the paper. It should feel firm and spring back.

Transfer the packets to warmed dinner plates and serve right away. Let each guest snip open his or her packet at the table, then slide the contents onto the plate. Pass a bowl for discarding the paper.

Tarragon lends its sweet anise notes to the buttery juices of mild-tasting chicken breasts baked in parchment paper. Spring's fresh English peas and newly harvested potatoes add substance and bright color to this simple, light, and fresh dish.

Newly harvested leeks offer a mild onionlike taste. Here, they are sautéed with fresh fennel in the brown drippings from a simple pan-roasted chicken. The result is a delicious vegetable sauce for the bird, enhanced by white wine and rich cream.

pan-roasted chicken with fennel, leeks, and cream

whole chicken, 1 (about 3½ pounds)

kosher salt and freshly ground pepper

peanut or grape seed oil, 1 tablespoon

unsalted butter, 3 tablespoons

fennel bulb, 1 (about 1 pound), cored and cut into ½-inch pieces

leeks, 3, white and pale green parts cut into ½-inch pieces

dry white wine, ¼ cup

heavy cream, 1 cup

fennel fronds, 2 tablespoons chopped

MAKES 4 SERVINGS

Preheat the oven to 400°F. Cut the chicken into 9 pieces (page 142), then season with 1½ teaspoons salt and ½ teaspoon pepper.

In a large ovenproof frying pan, heat the oil over medium-high heat until very hot but not smoking. Working in batches, add the chicken, skin side down, and cook, turning once, until golden brown on both sides, about 6 minutes per batch. Transfer to a platter. Pour off the fat from the pan. Return all of the chicken, skin side up, to the pan, place the pan in the oven, and roast until an instant-read thermometer inserted in the thickest part of the breast meat registers 170°F, about 30 minutes.

Transfer the chicken pieces to a platter and tent with aluminum foil to keep warm. Pour the pan juices into a liquid measuring cup, let stand for 2 minutes, and then skim the fat from the surface. Return the pan to the stove top over medium heat, add 2 tablespoons of the butter, and allow it to melt. Add the fennel and stir well to coat with the butter. Cover, reduce the heat to medium, and sauté until the fennel softens, about 5 minutes. Stir in the leeks and the remaining 1 tablespoon butter, cover, and cook, stirring occasionally, until the fennel is tender, about 5 minutes longer.

Stir in the wine and the cream. Pour the pan juices back into the pan. Raise the heat to high and boil until the liquid lightly coats the back of a spoon, about 3 minutes. Taste and adjust the seasonings.

Transfer the chicken to warmed dinner plates. Spoon some of the sauce over each serving and sprinkle with the fennel fronds. Serve right away.

Fennel has a mild licorice flavor that mellows and sweetens during cooking, and is well matched with delicate, onionlike leeks. Feathery fennel fronds are a fragrant and fitting garnish for any dish, like this one, with fennel as an ingredient. Cream draws the tastes of the fennel, leeks, and chicken together and creates a rich, velvety sauce.

stir-fried chicken with sugar snap peas, lemon zest, and mint

Mint leaves add a fresh, bracing quality to an easy chicken stir-fry of pure, simple flavors. Sugar snap peas provide their natural sweetness and irresistible crunch, while fragrant lemon zest and juice add a welcome brightness.

Cut the chicken breast halves across the grain on a slight diagonal into slices about ½ inch thick. Cut the slices lengthwise into strips about ½ inch wide. Season the chicken with 1 teaspoon salt and ¼ teaspoon pepper.

Finely grate the zest from the lemon, and then squeeze 2 tablespoons lemon juice. In a small nonreactive bowl, stir together the broth, fish sauce, sugar, and lemon zest and juice. In another small bowl, mix the cornstarch with 1 tablespoon cold water.

Heat a wok or very large frying pan over medium-high heat until hot. Add 2 tablespoons of the oil and swirl the pan to coat it well. Add the chicken and stir-fry until opaque throughout, about 3 minutes. Transfer to a platter.

Return the pan to medium-high heat, add the remaining 2 tablespoons oil, and heat until very hot but not smoking. Add the chopped green onion bottoms, ginger, and garlic and stir-fry until fragrant, about 15 seconds. Add the sugar snap peas and ¼ cup water, cover, and cook, stirring occasionally, until the sugar snaps turn a bright green color, about 1 minute.

Return the chicken to the pan, and then add the sliced green onion tops and chopped mint. Stir the broth mixture briefly to mix, add it into the pan, and bring to a boil, stirring constantly. Stir the cornstarch mixture briefly to mix, stir it into the pan, and cook until the sauce is slightly thickened, about 15 seconds. Taste and adjust the seasonings.

Transfer to a warmed deep serving dish and serve right away.

boneless, skinless chicken breast halves, 2 (about 6 ounces each)

kosher salt and freshly ground pepper

lemon, 1

low-sodium chicken broth or stock, 1 cup

asian fish sauce, 2 tablespoons

sugar, 1 teaspoon

cornstarch, 1 teaspoon

canola oil, 4 tablespoons

green onions, 2, white and pale green bottoms chopped, green tops thinly sliced

fresh ginger, one ½-inch piece, peeled and minced

garlic, 2 cloves, minced

sugar snap peas, ½ pound

fresh mint, 3 tablespoons coarsely chopped

MAKES 4–6 SERVINGS

baked stuffed chicken breasts with arugula and fontina

extra-virgin olive oil,
2 tablespoons, plus oil for the baking dish

fontina cheese, preferably fontina val d'aosta,
5 ounces

boneless, skinless chicken breast halves, 4 (about 7 ounces each)

kosher salt and freshly ground pepper

garlic, 1 large clove, minced

arugula leaves, 16, tough stems removed

large eggs, 2

panko bread crumbs, 1 cup

dried oregano, 1 teaspoon

dried rosemary,
1 teaspoon, crumbled

lemon, 1, cut into 8 wedges

MAKES 4 SERVINGS

Position a rack in the upper third of the oven and preheat to 400°F. Line a baking sheet with parchment paper. Lightly oil a 9-by-13-inch baking dish. Trim off and discard the rind from the cheese. Cut the cheese into four 2-by-1½-inch rectangles about ⅛ inch thick.

Using a flat meat pounder, pound each chicken breast half until flattened to an even thickness of about ¼ inch. Season the chicken breasts with 1½ teaspoons salt and ½ teaspoon pepper.

Position 1 pounded chicken breast, with the long side facing you, on the work surface. Top with one-fourth of the garlic followed by 4 arugula leaves, torn as needed to fit the breast half, leaving a 1-inch border uncovered on all sides. Top with a piece of cheese. Starting at a short end, roll up the breast, tucking in the arugula as needed; set seam side down. Repeat with the remaining chicken, garlic, arugula, and cheese.

In a medium bowl, whisk together the eggs and 1 tablespoon of the oil. In a shallow dish, stir together the bread crumbs, oregano, and rosemary. One at a time, coat a rolled chicken breast with the egg mixture then roll in the bread crumbs, coating evenly. Place the breaded breasts seam side down on the parchment-lined baking sheet.

Place the oiled baking dish in the oven and heat until very hot, about 3 minutes. Carefully arrange the breaded breasts, seam side down, in the hot dish. Drizzle evenly with the remaining 1 tablespoon oil. Bake until the bread crumbs are golden brown and an instant-read thermometer inserted in the center of a stuffed breast registers 170°F, 25–35 minutes.

Transfer the chicken to a carving board. Cut each stuffed breast crosswise into slices about ½ inch thick and transfer to warmed dinner plates. Serve right away. Pass the lemon wedges at the table.

Arugula has a peppery, slightly bitter bite and a delicate, tender texture. In this simple stuffing, it is matched with fontina, which adds a richness and mild nuttiness. The panko coating cooks to a crisp, light finish in the hot oven, delivering a perfect counterpoint to the creamy melted cheese at the heart of each roll.

Fresh morels are a prized ingredient, available only for a short time. Paired with fresh herbs to bring out their woodsy quality, and offset by the tang of a crème fraîche–enriched sauce, they help create a quintessential springtime chicken dish.

chicken fricassee with morel mushrooms and thyme

fresh morel mushrooms,
¾ pound, each cut in half lengthwise

whole chicken, 1 (about 3½ pounds)

kosher salt and freshly ground pepper

peanut or grape seed oil, 1 teaspoon

unsalted butter, 4 tablespoons

shallots, 2, minced

all-purpose flour, 3 tablespoons

dry white wine, ¾ cup

low-sodium chicken broth or stock, 1½ cups

fresh thyme, 4 sprigs

fresh flat-leaf parsley, 4 sprigs

crème fraîche (page 145 or purchased), ½ cup

fresh chives, 1 tablespoon minced

MAKES 4 SERVINGS

Rinse the morels quickly but thoroughly under cold running water, taking care to dislodge any grit caught in their spongelike crevices. Pat dry.

Cut the chicken into 9 pieces (page 142), then season with 1½ teaspoons salt and ½ teaspoon pepper.

In a Dutch oven or other heavy pot with a lid, heat the oil over medium-high heat until very hot but not smoking. Working in batches, add the chicken pieces, skin side down, and cook, turning once or twice, until lightly browned on both sides, about 5 minutes per batch. Transfer to a platter.

Reduce the heat to medium, add 2 tablespoons of the butter, and allow it to melt. Add half of the morels and sauté until they give off their juices, the juices evaporate, and the mushrooms are sizzling, about 6 minutes. During the last 2 minutes or so, stir in half of the shallots. Transfer the mixture to a plate. Repeat with the remaining butter, morels, and shallots.

Return the morel mixture to the Dutch oven over medium-low heat, sprinkle with the flour, and mix well. Stir in the wine and broth and bring to a simmer. Gather the thyme and parsley sprigs, tie together with kitchen string, and add to the pot. Return the drumsticks, thighs, and wings, then the breasts to the pot. Cover and simmer, stirring the sauce and turning the chicken occasionally, until the chicken shows no sign of pink when pierced with a sharp knife near the bone, 35–40 minutes.

Transfer the chicken to a warmed deep serving dish and tent with aluminum foil. Discard the herb sprigs. Stir the crème fraîche into the pot, raise the heat to medium-high, and bring to a boil. Cook, stirring often, until the sauce is thickened and coats the spoon, about 5 minutes. Taste and adjust the seasonings. Pour the sauce over the chicken, sprinkle with the chives, and serve right away.

The herbal, woodsy flavor of fresh thyme amplifies the meaty, musky taste of morel mushrooms. In this earthy, savory version of a classic French chicken dish, the morels' unique character is showcased in a creamy, tangy, crème fraîche–based sauce.

seared five-spice duck breasts with rhubarb compote

Chinese five-spice powder, a blend of warm, fragrant spices, seasons meaty duck breasts, giving them an exotic, intriguing flavor. A cinnamon-spiced sweet and tart rhubarb compote made with fresh orange juice and brown sugar pairs well with the rich, rosy meat of the duck.

Using a sharp, thin-bladed knife, score the skin of each duck breast half in a crosshatch pattern. Stir together the five-spice powder, 1 teaspoon salt, and ½ teaspoon pepper and season the duck breasts on both sides with the mixture. Let stand at room temperature for 30 minutes.

Finely grate the zest from the orange, then squeeze ½ cup orange juice, adding water to supplement, if needed. In a heavy nonreactive saucepan over medium heat, combine the orange zest and juice, rhubarb, brown sugar, and cinnamon. Bring to a boil, stirring often. Reduce the heat to medium-low and simmer, stirring occasionally, until the rhubarb is just tender, about 8 minutes.

Meanwhile, fill a large bowl with ice water. When the rhubarb is ready, using a slotted spoon, transfer it to a heatproof bowl and nest the bowl in the ice water bath. Raise the heat to high and boil the juices in the pan until syrupy, about 5 minutes. Pour the juices over the rhubarb, discard the cinnamon, and stir gently. Let cool while preparing the duck.

Place the duck breasts, skin side down, in a very large frying pan. Place the frying pan over medium-high heat. Cook until the skin is golden brown and the duck has rendered a good amount of fat, about 7 minutes. Transfer the duck to a large plate and pour off the fat from the pan. Return the pan to medium-high heat, and then return the duck breasts, skin side up, to the pan. Cook until the undersides are nicely browned, about 7 minutes longer for medium-rare or until cooked to your liking.

Transfer the duck to a carving board and let rest for 5 minutes. Cut each breast half across the grain into slices about ½ inch thick and transfer to warmed dinner plates. Spoon the compote onto each plate, and serve right away. Pass the remaining compote at the table.

boneless duck breast halves, 4 (about 7 ounces each)

chinese five-spice powder, 1 teaspoon

kosher salt and freshly ground pepper

orange, 1 large

rhubarb stalks, 4 or 5 (about 10 ounces total weight), cut into ½-inch pieces

light brown sugar, ½ cup firmly packed

cinnamon stick, 3-inch piece

MAKES 4 SERVINGS

thai green curry with chicken and asparagus

sea salt

asparagus, 1½ pounds

boneless, skinless chicken breast halves, 4 (about 6 ounces each)

peanut or grape seed oil, 2 tablespoons

yellow onion, 1, cut into 8 wedges

red bell pepper, 1 small, cut into 1½-by-¼-inch strips

fresh ginger, one ½-inch piece, peeled and minced

garlic, 2 cloves, minced

unsweetened coconut milk, 1 can (14 ounces)

thai green curry paste, 3 tablespoons

low-sodium chicken broth or stock, 1 cup

asian fish sauce, 2 tablespoons

thai basil, ½ cup loosely packed small leaves

lime, 1, cut into 8 wedges

MAKES 4–6 SERVINGS

Bring a saucepan of lightly salted water to a boil over high heat. While the water is heating, snap the tough stems off of the asparagus spears and cut the spears into 2-inch lengths. Add the asparagus to the boiling water and cook just until tender-crisp, about 2 minutes. Drain well and rinse under cold running water until cool. Pat dry.

Cut the chicken breast halves across the grain on a slight diagonal into slices about ½ inch thick. Cut the slices vertically into strips about ½ inch wide. Season the chicken strips with 1 teaspoon salt.

Heat a very large frying pan over medium-high heat until hot. Add the oil and swirl the pan to coat it well. Add the onion and bell pepper and sauté until beginning to soften, about 3 minutes. Stir in the ginger and garlic and sauté until fragrant, about 30 seconds. Transfer the mixture to a plate.

Open the can of coconut milk (do not shake it) and scoop out 3 tablespoons of the thick coconut cream on the top. Return the frying pan to medium-high heat. Add the coconut cream and curry paste to the frying pan and stir well. Whisk in the remaining coconut cream and milk, the broth, and fish sauce. Return the vegetable mixture to the pan, stir in the chicken strips, and bring to a boil. Reduce the heat to medium-low and simmer briskly, stirring occasionally, until the sauce has reduced slightly and the vegetables are tender-crisp, about 5 minutes. Stir in the asparagus and cook until the chicken is opaque throughout and the asparagus is heated through, about 3 minutes. Taste and adjust the seasonings.

Scatter the basil over the curry. Divide the curry evenly among warmed bowls and serve right away. Pass the lime wedges at the table.

Thai green curry paste has an incredibly bold, concentrated taste as well as spicy heat. Here, it is tempered by rich, creamy coconut milk. A sprinkle of fragrant Thai basil over the curry just before serving adds a freshness that perks up all of the complex flavors in the dish.

Toasted and hand-crushed, North African spices bring unmatched flavor to a marinade for grilled chicken pieces, which is made by puréeing smoky roasted red peppers with aromatic ingredients. A measure of spicy harissa adds punch.

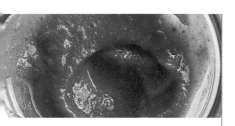

harissa-marinated grilled chicken

In this dish, chicken is treated with a marinade that is boldly accented with harissa, a fiery Morroccan spice paste. Toasted coriander, with its hints of lemon and caraway, and musky, intense cumin add their fragrance and complexity to the flavorful dish. Cooking on a hot grill adds a smokiness that works well with all of the robust seasonings.

Toast the cumin and coriander seeds (page 144) and pour onto a plate to cool. Using a mortar and pestle or a spice grinder, finely grind the spices.

Position an oven or broiler rack about 6 inches from the heat source and preheat the broiler. Place the peppers on a rimmed baking sheet and broil, turning the peppers occasionally, until the skins are charred, about 8 minutes. Transfer to a plate and let cool. Remove and discard the skins, seeds, ribs, and stems. In a food processor, combine the peppers, spice mixture, lemon juice, onion, garlic, harissa, and salt. With the motor running, add the olive oil in a slow, steady stream and process to a smooth purée. Pour half of this pepper mixture into a large nonreactive bowl.

Cut the chicken into 9 pieces (page 142). Add the chicken pieces to the bowl with the pepper mixture, turn the pieces to coat evenly, and then cover the bowl. Pour the remaining pepper mixture into a small nonreactive bowl and cover. Refrigerate both bowls for at least 2 hours and up to 8 hours. Remove the bowls from the refrigerator and let stand at room temperature for 1 hour before grilling the chicken.

Prepare a charcoal or gas grill for indirect-heat cooking over high heat (page 143 or 144). Replace the grill grate and brush it with canola oil.

Remove the chicken from its bowl, allowing the marinade to cling. Discard the marinade. Place the chicken, skin side down, on the cool side of the grill. Cover the grill and cook the chicken, basting occasionally with the pepper mixture in the small bowl, for 20 minutes. Turn the chicken pieces over and continue to cook, covered and basting occasionally, until an instant-read thermometer inserted in the thickest part of the breast meat registers 170°F, about 20 minutes longer.

Transfer the chicken to a warmed platter and serve right away.

cumin seeds, 2 teaspoons

coriander seeds, 2 teaspoons

red bell peppers, 2

fresh lemon juice, 1/3 cup

yellow onion, 1, coarsely chopped

garlic, 4 cloves, coarsely chopped

harissa, 2 tablespoons

kosher salt, 2 teaspoons

extra-virgin olive oil, 1/2 cup

whole chicken, 1 (about 4 pounds)

canola oil for grilling

MAKES 4 SERVINGS

summer

grilled chicken with corn and smoked mozzarella salad

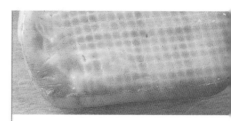

whole chicken, 1 (about 4 pounds)

extra-virgin olive oil, ¼ cup plus 1 tablespoon

kosher salt and freshly ground pepper

fresh sweet corn, 2 ears

canola oil for grilling

white balsamic vinegar, 1 tablespoon

garlic, 1 clove, minced

smoked mozzarella cheese, ½ pound, cut into ½-inch cubes

cherry tomatoes, 1 cup, halved

fresh basil leaves, 3 tablespoons roughly torn

MAKES 4 SERVINGS

Pull off the fat from around the chicken's cavity and discard the fat. Brush the chicken all over with the 1 tablespoon olive oil. Season the chicken, inside and out, with 1½ teaspoons salt and ½ teaspoon pepper. Let the chicken stand at room temperature while preparing the grill. Remove the husks and silk from the corn and wrap each ear in aluminum foil.

Prepare a charcoal or gas grill for indirect-heat cooking over high heat (page 143 or 144). Replace the grill grate and brush it with canola oil.

Place the chicken, breast side up, on the cool side of the grill. Place the foil-wrapped corn on the hot side of the grill. Cover the grill and cook the corn, turning occasionally, until the kernels are lightly toasted (open the foil to check), about 15 minutes. Transfer the corn to a plate, unwrap the ears, and let cool. Continue to cook the chicken, covered, until an instant-read thermometer inserted in the thickest part of the breast meat registers 170°F, about 1 hour longer.

Meanwhile, when the corn is cool enough to handle, use a large, sharp knife to carefully cut the ears in half crosswise. One at a time, stand the halves, flat end down, on a cutting board and cut the kernels from the cob.

In a serving bowl, whisk together the vinegar, garlic, ½ teaspoon salt, and ¼ teaspoon pepper. Gradually whisk in the ¼ cup olive oil. Add the corn, mozzarella, cherry tomatoes, and basil and mix gently. Taste and adjust the seasonings. Set aside at room temperature to blend the flavors while the chicken finishes cooking.

When the chicken is ready, transfer to a carving board and let rest for 10 minutes. Carve the chicken and serve right away with the salad.

Smoked mozzarella has a firm, creamy texture that pairs well with the other ingredients in this chunky, colorful salad. Its flavor bolsters the smokiness of the grilled corn and grill-roasted chicken. Cherry tomatoes bring a juicy, sweet taste and basil adds a summery freshness.

grilled chicken skewers with habanero chile and allspice

Allspice tastes of cloves, cinnamon, and nutmeg combined. Its warm flavor blends with the fiery heat of habanero chile in this rendition of Jamaican jerk seasoning. The heat is tempered by fresh-tasting green onions, salty soy sauce, and sharp vinegar.

Cut the chile in half and remove and discard the seeds. Reserve half of the chile for another use (or use both halves if you like your food very spicy).

Turn on a food processor and drop the garlic and chile half through the feed tube to chop them. Stop the motor, add the green onions, vinegar, soy sauce, allspice, thyme, and salt and pulse a few times to finely chop the green onions. With the motor running, add the oil in a slow, steady stream and process until the mixture is smooth.

Cut each chicken breast into 8 pieces each about 1 inch square, to make a total of 24 pieces. Transfer the pieces to a nonreactive bowl. Pour in the marinade and stir to coat evenly. Cover and refrigerate for at least 4 hours and up to 6 hours.

Soak 6 bamboo skewers in water to cover for at least 30 minutes.

Prepare a charcoal or gas grill for direct-heat cooking over medium-high heat (page 143 or 144). Replace the grill grate and lightly oil it.

While the grill heats, drain the skewers. Remove the chicken from the marinade and discard the marinade. Thread 4 chicken pieces, alternating with 3 red pepper pieces, onto each skewer.

Place the skewers on the grill, cover, and cook, turning the skewers occasionally, until the chicken feels firm when pressed with a fingertip, 10–12 minutes total.

Transfer the skewers to a warmed platter and serve right away.

habanero chile, 1

garlic, 2 cloves

green onions, 6, coarsely chopped

cider vinegar, 2 tablespoons

soy sauce, 1 tablespoon

ground allspice, 1 teaspoon

dried thyme, 1 teaspoon

kosher salt, 1/2 teaspoon

canola oil, 1/2 cup, plus oil for grilling

boneless, skinless chicken breast halves, 3 (about 7 ounces each)

red bell pepper, 1 large, cut into 1-inch squares

MAKES 3–4 SERVINGS

Fresh peaches and bourbon, both iconic ingredients in the cooking of the American South, combine in a new twist on barbecue sauce. Chicken pieces are grilled over hickory chips, whose smoky taste contrasts with the zesty, sweet-sour sauce and mild poultry.

grilled chicken with peach-bourbon barbecue sauce

The wood-aged character of bourbon adds toasty molasses hints to a unique barbecue sauce made with fruity, ripe, yellow summer peaches. A savory spice rub and fragrant smoke from hickory wood chips infuse the chicken with layers of flavor. The result is an irresistibly succulent "barbecued" chicken.

In a bowl, soak the hickory chips in cold water to cover for at least 30 minutes or up to 2 hours. Bring a saucepan three-fourths full of water to a boil over high heat. Add the peaches and heat just until the skins loosen, about 30 seconds. Drain and rinse under cold running water. Peel, halve, and pit the peaches and then coarsely chop.

In a nonreactive saucepan over medium heat, heat 2 tablespoons of the oil. Add the onion and sauté until golden, about 6 minutes. Stir in the garlic and sauté until fragrant, about 1 minute. Stir in the peaches, ketchup, sugar, bourbon, vinegar, and mustard and bring to a simmer. Reduce the heat to medium-low and simmer uncovered, stirring often, until slightly thickened, about 25 minutes. Transfer to a bowl and stir in the hot sauce. Let cool.

Cut the chicken into 9 pieces (page 142). In a small bowl, stir together the paprika, 2 teaspoons salt, ½ teaspoon pepper, the garlic powder, and onion powder. Season the chicken pieces with the paprika mixture. Brush the chicken with the remaining 2 tablespoons oil and let stand at room temperature while the grill heats. Drain the hickory chips.

Prepare a charcoal or gas grill for indirect-heat cooking over high heat (page 143 or 144). Sprinkle the drained wood chips over the coals or use a wood-chip smoker box on the gas grill. Replace the grill grate and lightly oil it.

Place the chicken, skin side down, on the cool side of the grill. Cover the grill and cook the chicken for 20 minutes. Turn the chicken over and continue to cook, covered, until an instant-read thermometer inserted in the thickest part of the breast meat registers 170°F, about 20 minutes longer; during the last 5–10 minutes, brush the chicken pieces with the peach sauce and cook, turning once or twice, until glazed.

Transfer to a warmed platter and serve right away.

hickory chips, 1 cup

yellow peaches, 2

canola oil, 4 tablespoons, plus oil for grilling

yellow onion, 1, chopped

garlic, 2 cloves, finely chopped

organic ketchup, 1 cup

light brown sugar, ½ cup firmly packed

bourbon, ⅓ cup

cider vinegar, ¼ cup

dijon mustard, 2 tablespoons

red hot-pepper sauce, 2 teaspoons

whole chicken, 1 (about 4 pounds)

spanish smoked paprika, 2 teaspoons

kosher salt and freshly ground pepper

garlic powder, ½ teaspoon

onion powder, ½ teaspoon

MAKES 4 SERVINGS

buttermilk-and-herb fried chicken

buttermilk, 1 quart

table salt, ⅓ cup plus ½ teaspoon

red hot-pepper sauce, 1 tablespoon

dried marjoram, 1 teaspoon

dried rubbed sage, 1 teaspoon

dried thyme, 1 teaspoon

dried rosemary, 1 teaspoon, crumbled

whole chicken, 1 (about 3½ pounds)

all-purpose flour, 1⅓ cups

baking powder, 1 teaspoon

freshly ground pepper, ½ teaspoon

canola oil for frying

MAKES 4 SERVINGS

In a large nonreactive bowl, whisk together the buttermilk, the ⅓ cup salt, hot sauce, marjoram, sage, thyme, and rosemary until blended and the salt is dissolved.

Cut the chicken into 9 pieces (page 142), then cut each breast half in half crosswise. Add the chicken pieces to the buttermilk mixture, submerging them fully. Cover and refrigerate for at least 6 hours and up to 8 hours.

Preheat the oven to 400°F. Line a rimmed baking sheet with parchment paper. In a shallow bowl, whisk together the flour, baking powder, the ½ teaspoon salt, and pepper. Remove the chicken from the buttermilk mixture; discard the buttermilk mixture. One piece at a time, dip the chicken in the flour mixture, coating evenly and shaking off the excess flour. Transfer the chicken to the prepared baking sheet.

Pour the oil to a depth of ½ inch into a large, heavy frying pan (preferably cast iron) and heat over medium-high heat until very hot but not smoking. Add the wings, thighs, and drumsticks to the oil and fry until golden brown, about 5 minutes. Carefully turn and cook until the second sides are golden brown, about 5 minutes longer. Transfer to a clean rimmed baking sheet and bake for 10 minutes.

Meanwhile, fry the chicken breast pieces in the hot oil in the same manner. Remove the baking sheet from the oven, add the chicken breasts to it, and then return the pan to the oven and continue to bake all of the pieces until an instant-read thermometer inserted in the thickest part of the breast meat registers 170°F, about 10 minutes longer.

Drain the chicken pieces on paper towels for just a minute or two, then transfer to a warmed platter and serve right away.

Soaking the chicken in seasoned buttermilk flavors the meat right down to the bone and ensures that it stays tender and moist after frying. With every bite, you'll taste the tangy buttermilk, robust herbs, and a hint of spicy heat from the pepper sauce.

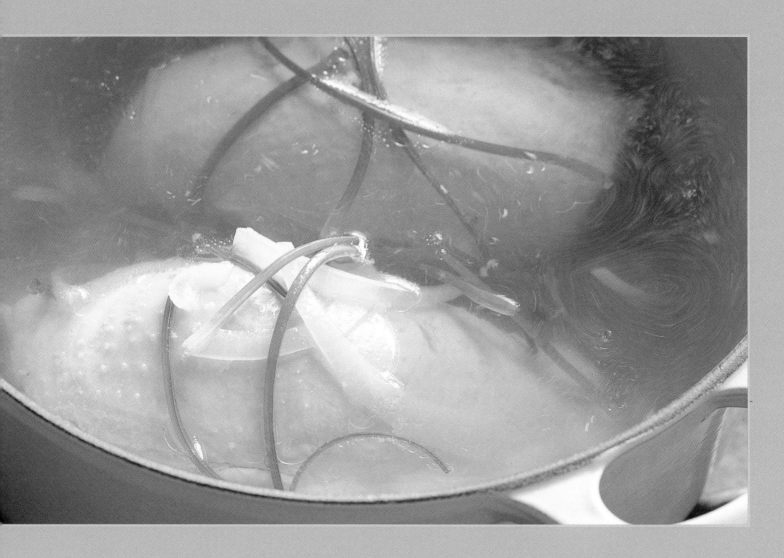

Here, mild chicken breasts are gently poached in an aromatic broth, then shredded and made into a main-course salad of tart multicolored tomatoes, meaty black beans, and zesty seasonings. It's a perfect, light dish for summer.

chicken salad with tomatoes, black beans, and cilantro

white onion, 1

fresh cilantro, ¼ bunch

bone-in, skin-on chicken breast halves, 2 (about ¾ pound each)

garlic, 2 cloves, crushed, plus 1 clove, minced

kosher salt and freshly ground pepper

fresh lime juice, 2 tablespoons

jalapeño chile, 1, seeded and minced

extra-virgin olive oil, ⅓ cup

heirloom tomatoes, 2, preferably 1 red and 1 yellow or green, seeded and cut into ½-inch dice

canned black beans, 1 cup, rinsed and drained

butter or bibb lettuce, 1 head, separated into leaves

MAKES 4–6 SERVINGS

Cut the onion in half lengthwise. Cut half of the onion into thin half moon–shaped slices. Finely chop the remaining half and measure ¼ cup. Pluck the leaves from the cilantro sprigs; reserve both the stems and leaves.

Place the chicken breasts in a large saucepan and add the cilantro stems, onion slices, crushed garlic, and 1 teaspoon salt. Add water to barely cover the chicken. Bring to a boil over high heat, skimming off any foam that rises to the surface. Reduce the heat to low and simmer, partially covered, for 20 minutes. Remove the pan from the heat. Cover and let stand until a breast shows no sign of pink when pierced with the tip of a sharp knife near the bone, about 15 minutes. Transfer the chicken to a plate and let cool. (Discard the stock or save for another use.)

Remove and discard the skin and bones from the chicken breasts and shred the meat into bite-sized pieces. Coarsely chop the reserved cilantro leaves (you should have about 2 tablespoons).

In a nonreactive bowl, combine the lime juice, half of the minced jalapeño, the minced garlic, ½ teaspoon salt, and ¼ teaspoon pepper. Gradually whisk in the olive oil. Add the chicken, tomatoes, chopped onion, chopped cilantro, and black beans. Mix gently to combine. Taste and adjust the seasonings, and then add as much of the remaining jalapeño as needed to achieve the desired spiciness. Cover and refrigerate to chill slightly, at least 20 minutes or up to 2 hours.

Arrange a couple of lettuce leaves on each plate. Spoon some of the salad on top and serve right away.

The bold taste of cilantro contains hints of citrus, pepper, and herbaceous green grass. In this recipe, cilantro stems season the chicken cooking liquid and the leaves are tossed into the salad. The mild flavor of the chicken and black beans are sharpened by ripe heirloom tomatoes and tart lime juice for a bright, tasty summer dish.

grilled chicken with plum-jalapeño relish

A lightly spicy, sweet-tart fresh plum relish——use whatever plum variety is ripe and flavorful——adds dimension to chicken cooked on a hot grill. The warm, citrusy fragrance of toasted coriander seeds and the pepperiness of fresh ginger act as a bridge between the smoky nuances of the grilled chicken and the fruity taste of the relish.

In a saucepan, combine half of the plums with the onion, ginger, chile, garlic, and sugar. Bring to a boil over medium heat, stirring often. Reduce the heat to medium-low, cover, and cook, stirring occasionally, until the plums have broken down into a sauce, about 15 minutes. Stir in the remaining plums and cook just until they are heated through, about 3 minutes. Meanwhile, fill a large bowl with ice water. When the plum relish is ready, transfer it to a heatproof bowl and nest the bowl in the ice water bath. Let cool in the ice bath while preparing the chicken.

Toast the coriander seeds (page 144) and pour onto to a plate to cool. Using a mortar and pestle or a spice grinder, finely grind the coriander. In a small bowl, stir together the ground coriander, 1½ teaspoons salt, and ½ teaspoon pepper. Cut the chicken into 9 pieces (page 142). Brush the chicken pieces with the olive oil, then season with the coriander mixture.

Prepare a charcoal or gas grill for indirect-heat cooking over high heat (page 143 or 144). Replace the grill grate and brush it with canola oil.

Arrange the chicken pieces, skin side down, on the grill grate on the cool side of the grill. Cover the grill and cook the chicken for 20 minutes. Turn the chicken pieces over and continue to cook, covered, until an instant-read thermometer inserted in the thickest part of the breast meat registers 170°F, about 20 minutes longer.

Meanwhile, season the cooled plum relish to taste with salt, and then transfer to a serving bowl.

When the chicken is ready, transfer the pieces to a warmed serving platter and serve right away. Pass the relish at the table.

plums, 2 large (¾ pound total weight), halved, pitted, and cut into 1-inch pieces

small yellow onion, ½ cup finely chopped

fresh ginger, one 1-inch piece, peeled and minced

jalapeño chile, 1, seeded and minced

garlic, 1 clove, minced

light brown sugar, ⅓ cup firmly packed

coriander seeds, 2 teaspoons

kosher salt and freshly ground pepper

whole chicken, 1 (about 4 pounds)

extra-virgin olive oil, 1 tablespoon

canola oil for grilling

MAKES 4 SERVINGS

grilled butterflied chicken with chimichurri

fresh flat-leaf parsley leaves, 1 cup packed

fresh oregano leaves, ¼ cup packed

garlic, 3 cloves

green onions, 2, coarsely chopped

red wine vinegar, 2 tablespoons

red pepper flakes, ¼ teaspoon

kosher salt

extra-virgin olive oil, ½ cup plus 1 tablespoon

canola oil for grilling

whole chicken, 1 (about 4 pounds)

freshly ground pepper, ½ teaspoon

MAKES 4 SERVINGS

Finely chop enough parsley and oregano to make 1 tablespoon of each and reserve the chopped herbs for the chicken.

To make the chimichurri, turn on a food processor and drop 2 of the garlic cloves through the feed tube to chop them. Stop the motor, add the remaining parsley and oregano leaves and the green onions, and then pulse to coarsely chop. Add the vinegar, red pepper flakes, and ½ teaspoon salt. With the motor running, add the ½ cup olive oil in a slow, steady stream until the sauce is thick but pourable. Transfer the chimichurri to a serving bowl, taste, and adjust the seasoning with salt. Cover and let stand at room temperature while preparing the chicken.

Prepare a charcoal or gas grill for indirect-heat cooking over high heat (page 143 or 144). Replace the grill grate and lightly oil it.

While the grill heats, butterfly the chicken (page 143). Finely chop the remaining garlic clove. In a small bowl, mix the garlic with the reserved chopped parsley and oregano, 1 teaspoon salt, and the pepper. Brush the chicken with the remaining 1 tablespoon olive oil and rub the entire surface with the garlic-herb mixture.

Place the chicken, skin side down, on the grill grate on the cool side of the grill. Place a heavy cast-iron frying pan on top of the chicken. Cover the grill and cook the chicken for 20 minutes. Remove the frying pan and turn the chicken over, but do not replace the pan. Continue to cook, covered, until an instant-read thermometer inserted in the thickest part of the breast meat registers 170°F, about 40 minutes longer.

Transfer the chicken to a carving board and let rest for 5 minutes. Cut the chicken into quarters, spoon some of the chimichurri over each piece, and serve right away. Pass the remaining chimichurri at the table.

Make chimichurri, a lush, bright-green Argentinian condiment, when the herb garden is in full flush to show off the primary components: verdant flat-leaf parsley and earthy oregano. Garlic, green onions, vinegar, and red pepper flakes all add a pleasing kick to the fresh-tasting sauce that's a perfect accompaniment to grilled chicken.

Tart fresh cherries
are delicious with
dark-meat poultry.
Here, chicken
thighs are rubbed
with a mixture of
thyme and sea salt,
then they're roasted
and served with
a thyme-infused
cherry compote.
Used twice, the
herb helps marry
the two elements
on the plate.

roasted chicken thighs with cherry-thyme compote

extra-virgin olive oil,
2 tablespoons, plus oil for
the pan

fresh thyme, 3 teaspoons
minced

**kosher salt and freshly
ground pepper**

**bone-in, skin-on chicken
thighs,** 8 (about 3¼ pounds
total weight)

shallot, 1 small, minced

fresh bing cherries,
1 pound, pitted and
coarsely chopped

balsamic vinegar,
2 tablespoons

light brown sugar,
2 tablespoons firmly
packed

MAKES 4 SERVINGS

Preheat the oven to 425°F. Lightly oil a large flameproof roasting pan.

In a small bowl, stir together 2 teaspoons of the thyme, 1½ teaspoons salt, and ½ teaspoon pepper. Brush the chicken thighs with the 2 tablespoons olive oil, and then season with the thyme mixture. Arrange the thighs, skin side up, in the prepared roasting pan.

Roast the chicken until the skin is golden brown and an instant-read thermometer inserted in the thickest part of the thigh meat registers 170°F, about 35 minutes.

When the chicken is ready, transfer it to a warmed serving platter and tent with aluminum foil to keep warm. Pour off all but 1 tablespoon of the fat from the pan. Place the pan on the stove top over medium-low heat. Add the shallot and cook, scraping up the browned bits on the pan bottom, until softened, about 1 minute. Add the cherries and cook, stirring often, until the cherries are warm and begin to give off their juices, about 2 minutes. Add the vinegar, sugar, and the remaining 1 teaspoon thyme and stir to dissolve the sugar. Remove from the heat, taste, and adjust the seasonings. Transfer the compote to a serving bowl.

Serve the chicken right away. Pass the compote at the table.

Here, fresh sweet cherries, a summer favorite, are lightly cooked to make a chunky compote flavored with herbal thyme and enriched with the chicken's pan juices. Balsamic vinegar and brown sugar add hints of caramel-like flavor. The compote's lively taste balances the rich flavor of the burnished-brown roasted chicken thighs.

miso-marinated grilled chicken breasts with toasted sesame

Salty, intensely flavored miso has a bold, almost meaty taste, with earthy, nutty nuances. In this recipe, miso teams up with mirin and sake to make a simple savory-sweet Japanese-influenced marinade for lean, mild chicken breasts.

Peel the ginger and shred it on the large holes of a box grater-shredder. Finely chop the white and pale green bottoms of the green onions. Reserve the green onion tops.

In a bowl, whisk together the miso, mirin, sake, sugar, ginger, green onion bottoms, and 2 tablespoons water until well combined. Transfer to a nonreactive shallow baking dish.

Using a flat meat pounder, pound each chicken breast half until flattened to an even thickness of about ¼ inch. Place the chicken breasts in the miso mixture and turn to coat evenly. Cover and refrigerate for at least 2 hours and up to 6 hours.

While the chicken is marinating, toast the sesame seeds (page 144) and pour onto a plate to cool. Fill a bowl with ice water. Cut the reserved green onion tops lengthwise into thin ribbons, place them in the ice water so that they curl, and set aside.

Prepare a charcoal or gas grill for direct-heat cooking over medium-high heat (page 143 or 144). Replace the grill grate and lightly oil it.

Lift each chicken breast half from the miso mixture, and shake gently to remove the excess marinade. Place the breasts on the grill, cover, and cook, turning occasionally, until they spring back when pressed in the center, about 8 minutes total. Meanwhile, drain the green onion curls and pat dry.

Transfer the chicken to a warmed serving platter. Sprinkle with the green onion curls and sesame seeds. Serve right away.

fresh ginger, one 1-inch piece

green onions, 2

white miso, ½ cup

mirin, 3 tablespoons

sake, 3 tablespoons

sugar, 1 tablespoon

boneless, skinless chicken breast halves, 4 (about 6 ounces each)

sesame seeds, 2 tablespoons

canola oil for grilling

MAKES 4 SERVINGS

duck tacos with nectarine salsa

nectarines, 1 pound

lime, 1

red onion, 3 tablespoons finely chopped

jalapeño chile, 1, seeded and minced

honey, 1 tablespoon

kosher salt

boneless duck breast halves, 2 (about 7 ounces each)

chili powder, 2 teaspoons

romaine lettuce, 2 large leaves, finely shredded

corn tortillas, 8, warmed

MAKES 4 SERVINGS

Halve and pit the nectarines, and then cut them into ¾-inch pieces. Finely grate the zest from the lime, and then squeeze 1 tablespoon lime juice. In a nonreactive bowl, combine the nectarines, lime zest and juice, onion, chile, and honey and mix gently. Season to taste with salt. Cover and let stand at room temperature at least 30 minutes and up to 2 hours.

Using a sharp, thin-bladed knife, score the skin of each duck breast half in a crosshatch pattern. In a small bowl, stir together the chili powder and 1 teaspoon salt. Season the duck breasts with the chili powder mixture. Let stand at room temperature for 30 minutes.

Place the duck breasts, skin side down, in a large frying pan. Place the frying pan over medium-high heat. Cook until the skin is golden brown and the duck has rendered a good amount of fat, about 7 minutes. Transfer the duck to a plate and pour off the fat from the pan. Return the pan to medium-high heat, and then return the duck breasts, skin side up, to the pan. Cook until the undersides are nicely browned, about 7 minutes more for medium-rare.

Transfer the duck to a carving board and let rest for 5 minutes.

Cut each duck breast half across the grain into slices about ½ inch thick and transfer to a warmed platter. Serve right away with the salsa, shredded lettuce, and tortillas. Invite each guest to fill tortillas with sliced duck, some lettuce, and spoonfuls of salsa.

Floral, honeyed summer-ripe nectarines create a chunky salsa made piquant with red onion, jalapeño chile, and lime juice and zest. The spritely salsa cuts through the richness of the chili powder—spiced duck in this elegant version of a rustic Mexican favorite.

The trio of ginger, garlic, and green onions is a fundamental flavor base in Chinese cuisine. Here, it forms the foundation for a hearty mixture of boldly seasoned ground chicken to create a tasty filling for baked Asian eggplants.

asian eggplants stuffed with spicy minced chicken

Pine nuts have a buttery texture and a nutty, slightly resinous taste. They add richness and a touch of piney flavor to the sweet, savory, and spicy chicken filliing. Slender Asian eggplants are milder and more tender than their globe-shaped cousins, making them the perfect canvas for the layers of textures and tastes in this dish.

In a large frying pan over medium-high heat, warm 1 tablespoon of the oil. When the oil is very hot but not smoking, add the green onion bottoms, ginger, garlic, and chile. Stir-fry until fragrant, about 30 seconds, and then transfer to a large bowl. Rinse the pan, wipe dry, and set aside.

Add the chicken to a food processor and pulse until coarsely chopped. Scrape the chicken into the bowl with the green onion mixture. Add 2 tablespoons of the soy sauce, the hoisin sauce, and the pine nuts, and stir to combine. Trim off the top from each eggplant, then cut each eggplant in half lengthwise. Using the tip of a soup spoon, scrape out and discard most of the eggplant flesh, leaving shells a generous ¼ inch thick. Spoon the chicken into the eggplant halves, dividing it evenly.

In the frying pan, heat the remaining 2 tablespoons oil over medium-high heat until very hot but not smoking. Add the stuffed eggplants, stuffing side up, and cook until the undersides are lightly browned, about 1 minute. Pour the broth around the eggplants and cover the pan. Reduce the heat to medium-low and simmer until the eggplants are tender when pierced with the tip of a sharp knife, about 20 minutes.

Using a slotted spatula, transfer the eggplants to a warmed platter. In a small bowl, mix the remaining 2 tablespoons soy sauce, 2 tablespoons water, and the cornstarch. Stir the soy sauce–cornstarch mixture into the simmering broth in the pan and cook until lightly thickened, about 30 seconds. Taste and adjust the seasoning with soy sauce.

Spoon the sauce over the eggplants, sprinkle with red pepper flakes and the green onion tops, and serve right away.

canola oil, 3 tablespoons

green onions, 2, white and pale green bottoms chopped, green tops sliced

fresh ginger, one ½-inch piece, peeled and minced

garlic, 2 cloves, minced

serrano chile, 1, seeded and minced

boneless, skinless chicken thighs, 1 pound, cut into 1-inch chunks

soy sauce, 4 tablespoons, plus more as needed

hoisin sauce, 1 tablespoon

pine nuts, 2 tablespoons, toasted (page 144)

asian eggplants, 2, each about 10 inches long

low-sodium chicken broth or stock, ½ cup

cornstarch, 1½ teaspoons

red pepper flakes for garnish

MAKES 4 SERVINGS

fall

porter-braised chicken thighs with root vegetables

carrots, 2

red potatoes, 2

celery root, 1 (14 ounces)

yellow onion, 1 large

bone-in, skin-on chicken thighs, 8 (about 3¼ pounds total weight)

kosher salt and freshly ground pepper

canola oil, 2 tablespoons

unsalted butter, 7 tablespoons, at room temperature

porter, 2 bottles (12 ounces each)

low-sodium chicken broth or stock, 2 cups

light brown sugar, 2 tablespoons

dijon mustard, 2 tablespoons

tomato paste, 2 teaspoons

dried thyme, 1 teaspoon

all-purpose flour, ⅓ cup

MAKES 4 SERVINGS

Peel the carrots, and then cut the carrots and unpeeled potatoes into 1-inch chunks. Peel the celery root, cut in half lengthwise, and then cut away any spongy or gnarly parts. Cut into 1-inch chunks. Peel and chop the onion.

Season the chicken thighs with 2 teaspoons salt and ½ teaspoon pepper. In a Dutch oven or other heavy pot with a lid, heat the oil over medium-high heat until very hot but not smoking. Working in batches, add the chicken thighs, skin side down, and cook, turning once or twice, until lightly browned on both sides, about 5 minutes per batch. Transfer to a platter. Pour off the fat in the Dutch oven.

Reduce the heat to medium, add 2 tablespoons of the butter to the pot, and let it melt. Add the onion and sauté until golden, about 6 minutes. Add the carrots, potatoes, and celery root, and stir in the porter, broth, sugar, mustard, tomato paste, and thyme. Return the chicken thighs to the pot, submerging them in the liquid, and bring to a simmer. Cover, reduce the heat to medium-low, and simmer, stirring occasionally, for 30 minutes.

In a heatproof bowl, mash together the remaining 5 tablespoons butter and the flour to form a thick paste. Gradually whisk about 2 cups of the hot cooking liquid into the flour-butter mixture, and then stir this mixture into the pot. Cover and continue to simmer, stirring occasionally, until the chicken shows no sign of pink when pierced with the tip of a sharp knife near the bone, about 10 minutes longer. Taste and adjust the seasonings.

Divide the chicken, vegetables, and sauce among warmed deep bowls. Serve right away.

Slightly bitter and with a deep coffee-like flavor, porter, a very dark ale, makes this braise rustic and hearty. The interplay of the toasty nuances from the porter, the sweetness of root vegetables, and the spiciness of Dijon mustard creates a poultry stew full of contrasting, but harmonious, flavors.

maple-mustard turkey tenderloins with cranberry-port sauce

Sweet and slightly smoky maple syrup is an easy way to add full, complex flavor to both sweet and savory dishes. Here, it balances the spiciness of mustard to make a simple glaze for lean turkey tenderloins. A splash of full-bodied Port wine contributes to a bold sauce punctuated by sweet-and-sour fresh cranberries and zesty crystallized ginger.

Preheat the oven to 350°F. Using kitchen string, tie each tenderloin crosswise in 3 or 4 places, spacing the ties at even intervals. Season the tenderloins with 1 teaspoon salt and ½ teaspoon pepper.

In a large ovenproof frying pan over medium-high heat, melt the butter. Add the turkey and cook, turning occasionally, until browned on all sides, about 5 minutes total. Remove from the heat.

In a small bowl, stir together the maple syrup and mustard. Spread about half of the mixture over the tenderloins. Place the pan in the oven and cook for 10 minutes. Spread the remaining maple syrup mixture over the tenderloins, return to the oven, and continue to cook until an instant-read thermometer inserted in the center of a tenderloin registers 165°F, about 10 minutes longer.

While the turkey is roasting, in a heavy nonreactive saucepan, combine the cranberries, Port, sugar, and crystallized ginger and bring to a boil over high heat, stirring often. Reduce the heat to medium and cook, uncovered, at a brisk simmer, stirring often, until the berries have popped and the juices are syrupy, about 10 minutes. Meanwhile, fill a large bowl with ice water. When the sauce is ready, transfer it to a heatproof bowl and nest the bowl in the ice water bath. Let cool, then transfer to a serving bowl.

When the tenderloins are ready, transfer them to a carving board and let rest for 5 minutes. Snip the strings and cut the tenderloins crosswise into slices ½ inch thick.

Divide the turkey evenly among warmed dinner plates, fanning the slices. Spoon some of the cranberry sauce next to each portion and serve right away. Pass the remaining sauce at the table.

turkey tenderloins,
2 (about ¾ pound each)

kosher salt and freshly ground pepper

unsalted butter,
1 tablespoon

pure maple syrup,
2 tablespoons

dijon mustard,
1 tablespoon

fresh cranberries, 1¾ cups

tawny or ruby port, ½ cup

sugar, ½ cup

crystallized ginger,
3 tablespoons minced

MAKES 4–6 SERVINGS

Pomegranates lend their tart flavor to a creative spin on grilled chicken. The chicken pieces are first glazed with a mixture of wine and pomegranate juice, then they're sprinkled with pomegranate seeds for an appealing crunch.

pomegranate-glazed grilled chicken

Subtly sweet, slightly tart bottled pomegranate juice has a bright acidity and just a touch of fruitiness. It, along with robust red wine, forms the base of a garnet-colored glaze that complements smoky grilled chicken and yields a sumptuous burnished look. Fresh pomegranate seeds sprinkled on as a garnish echo the sweet-sour flavor of the glaze.

In a nonreactive saucepan over medium heat, melt the butter. Add the shallot and garlic and sauté until the shallot is softened, about 2 minutes. Stir in the pomegranate juice, wine, and sugar, raise the heat to high, and bring to a boil. Cook until reduced to ½ cup, about 10 minutes.

When the pomegranate mixture has reduced, in small bowl, mix the cornstarch and 1 tablespoon cold water. Stir the cornstarch mixture into the pomegranate mixture and cook just until thickened, about 10 seconds. Transfer to a small bowl and let cool.

Cut the chicken into 9 pieces (page 142), then brush with the olive oil. In a small bowl, stir together the oregano, cumin, 2 teaspoons salt, and ½ teaspoon pepper. Season the chicken pieces with the oregano mixture. Let stand at room temperature while the grill heats.

Prepare a charcoal or gas grill for indirect-heat cooking over high heat (page 143 or 144). Replace the grill grate and brush it with canola oil.

Place the chicken, skin side down, on the cool side of the grill. Cover the grill and cook the chicken for 20 minutes. Turn the chicken over and continue to cook, covered, until an instant-read thermometer inserted in the thickest part of the breast meat registers 165°F, about 15 minutes longer. Brush the skin side of the chicken with half of the pomegranate mixture and move, skin side down, to the hot side of the grill. Grill uncovered, turning occasionally and basting the other side with the remaining pomegranate mixture, until the chicken is glazed, about 5 minutes.

Transfer to a warmed platter, sprinkle with the pomegranate seeds, and serve right away.

unsalted butter,
1 tablespoon

shallot, 1, minced

garlic, 2 cloves, minced

bottled pomegranate juice,
¾ cup

hearty red wine, ¾ cup

light brown sugar, ¼ cup
firmly packed

cornstarch, 1 teaspoon

whole chicken, 1 (about
4 pounds)

extra-virgin olive oil,
1 tablespoon

dried oregano,
1½ teaspoons

ground cumin,
1½ teaspoons

**kosher salt and freshly
ground pepper**

canola oil for grilling

fresh pomegranate seeds,
⅓ cup

MAKES 4 SERVINGS

bacon-wrapped chicken breasts with warm lentil salad

lentils, preferably le puy,
1 cup

extra-virgin olive oil,
4 tablespoons

carrot, 1, peeled and cut
into ¼-inch dice

celery stalk, 1, cut into
¼-inch dice

shallot, 1, minced

garlic, 1 clove, minced

**low-sodium chicken broth
or stock,** 2 cups

**kosher salt and freshly
ground pepper**

bay leaf, 1

sherry vinegar,
1 tablespoon

fresh thyme, 1 teaspoon
minced

**boneless and skinless
chicken breast halves,**
4 (about 7 ounces each)

thick-cut bacon, 4 slices

MAKES 4 SERVINGS

Pick over the lentils, discarding any grit, and rinse well under running water.

In a saucepan over medium heat, warm 1 tablespoon of the oil. Add the carrot, celery, shallot, and garlic, cover, and cook, stirring occasionally, until the vegetables begin to soften, about 3 minutes. Stir in the lentils, broth, ½ teaspoon salt, ¼ teaspoon pepper, and the bay leaf. Raise the heat to high and bring to a boil. Reduce the heat to medium-low and simmer, uncovered, until the lentils are tender, about 45 minutes. If the liquid threatens to cook away before the lentils are done, add ¼ cup water. Remove from the heat and stir in 2 tablespoons of the oil, the vinegar, and the thyme. Taste and adjust the seasonings. Partially cover the pan and keep warm over very low heat. Preheat the oven to 375°F.

Using a flat meat pounder, pound each chicken breast half until flattened to an even thickness of about ¾ inch. Season the breasts with 1 teaspoon salt and ½ teaspoon pepper. With the smooth side of the breast facing up, and beginning at a point under the breast to hold the bacon in place, wrap a bacon strip around each breast in a spiral. If necessary, secure the bacon to the breast with a toothpick.

In a large, nonstick ovenproof frying pan over medium heat, warm the remaining 1 tablespoon oil. Add the chicken breasts, smooth sides up, and cook until lightly browned, about 2 minutes. Turn and cook until the second sides are lightly browned, about 3 minutes. Turn the breasts smooth side up and place the pan in the oven. Cook until an instant-read thermometer inserted in the thickest part of the breast meat registers 170°F and the bacon is browned, about 20 minutes.

Spoon the lentil salad into warmed shallow bowls. Top each portion with a chicken breast and serve right away.

Smoky bacon transforms mild-tasting chicken breasts into a hearty fall supper. Wrapped around each chicken breast, rich, fatty bacon adds flavor and keeps the flesh deliciously moist. The bacon also complements the warm salad of tiny green Le Puy lentils that have an earthy aroma and mild peppery taste.

The musky flavor of truffles is even more pronounced when paired with a rich ingredient. Here, they are used to create a flavorful layer under the skin of a roasted chicken. Later, more are swirled into a potent butter sauce to serve alongside the crisp, carved bird.

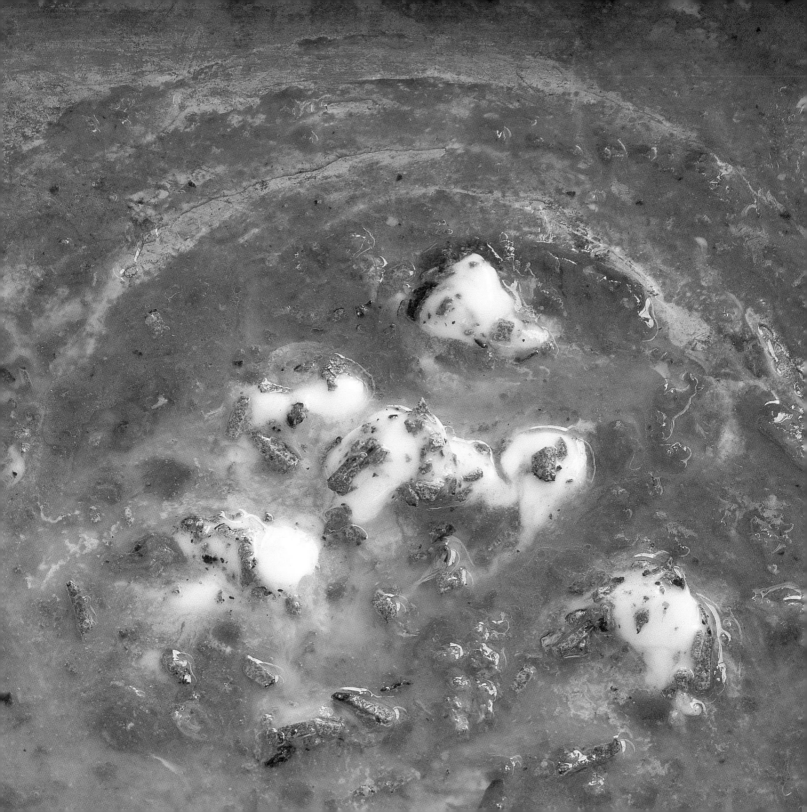

crisp-skin roasted chicken with truffle butter

whole chicken, 1 (about 4 pounds)

canola oil for the rack

homemade or prepared truffle butter (page 145 or purchased), 6 tablespoons, at room temperature

kosher salt and freshly ground pepper

onion, 1 small, cut into 2-inch pieces

small carrot, 1 small, cut into 2-inch pieces

small celery stalk, 1 small, cut into 2-inch pieces

low-sodium chicken broth or stock, 1 cup

MAKES 4 SERVINGS

Pull off the fat from around the chicken's cavity and coarsely chop the fat. In a small saucepan over low heat, cook the fat until rendered, about 15 minutes. Strain through a fine-mesh sieve; you should have about 1½ tablespoons fat. Let the chicken and fat stand at room temperature for 1–2 hours. Preheat the oven to 425°F. Place a V-shaped roasting rack in a flameproof roasting pan and lightly oil the rack.

Slip your fingers under the chicken skin and loosen the skin over the breast, thighs, and drumsticks. Slip about 4 tablespoons of the truffle butter under the skin and massage the chicken to distribute the butter evenly. Rub the rendered fat all over the exterior of the chicken and season the chicken inside and out with 2 teaspoons salt and ½ teaspoon pepper. Place the chicken on its side on the prepared rack in the pan. Roast for 20 minutes, then turn the chicken on its other side and roast for 20 minutes longer. Turn the chicken onto its back and add the onion, carrot, and celery to the pan. Continue to roast the chicken until golden brown and an instant-read thermometer inserted in the thickest part of the breast meat registers 170°F, 30–40 minutes. Tilt the chicken so any juice in the cavity flows into the pan. Transfer the chicken to a carving board and let rest for 10 minutes.

Using a slotted spoon, lift out and discard the vegetables. Pour the pan juices into a glass measuring cup, let stand for about 2 minutes, then use a spoon to skim the fat from the surface. Return the pan juices to the roasting pan and place the pan on the stove top over medium heat. Add the broth and bring to a boil, scraping up the browned bits from the pan bottom. Remove from the heat and whisk in the remaining truffle butter, 1 tablespoon at a time. Taste and adjust the seasonings.

Carve the chicken and arrange on warmed dinner plates. Pour some of the sauce over each serving and serve right away.

Distinctively earthy and intensely fragrant black truffles season this golden-brown roasted chicken. Truffle butter rubbed under the skin infuses the meat with flavor, and more butter whisked into a pan sauce made with the drippings gives the sauce a luscious, velvety feel and indulgent taste.

braised chicken with apples, cider, and brandy

Golden Delicious apples are a good choice here for a few reasons: they are sweet and juicy and they keep both their shape and butter-yellow color when cooked. Their flavor is intensified by the addition of two other ingredients, apple brandy and hard cider. Oniony leeks and woodsy fresh thyme lend a savory edge to balance the dish's sweetness.

Cut the chicken into 9 pieces (page 142). Season the chicken pieces with 1½ teaspoons salt and ½ teaspoon pepper.

In a Dutch oven or other heavy pot with a lid, heat the oil over medium-high heat until very hot but not smoking. Working in batches, add the chicken, skin side down, and cook, turning once or twice, until lightly browned on both sides, about 5 minutes per batch. Transfer to a platter.

Reduce the heat to medium, add 3 tablespoons of the butter to the pot and allow it to melt. Add the leeks, cover, and cook, stirring often, until tender, about 5 minutes. Stir in the flour followed by the cider, broth, and minced thyme and bring to a boil. Return the drumsticks, thighs, and wings, and then breasts to the pot. Cover, reduce the heat to medium-low, and simmer, stirring occasionally, for 30 minutes.

Meanwhile, peel and core the apples, cut them into wedges ½ inch thick, and place in a bowl. Sprinkle the lemon juice over the apples and toss to coat. In a large frying pan over medium-high heat, melt the remaining 1 tablespoon butter. Add the apples and sauté until the edges are golden, about 4 minutes. Carefully pour in the applejack and reduce the heat to low. Using a long-handled match, light the applejack and let the flame burn for 30 seconds, then cover to extinguish the flame.

After the chicken has simmered for 30 minutes, stir the apples into the pot with the chicken and continue to cook until the chicken shows no sign of pink when pierced with the tip of a knife near the bone, about 5 minutes. Taste and adjust the seasonings.

Spoon the chicken, apples, and sauce onto warmed dinner plates and garnish each serving with thyme sprigs. Serve right away.

whole chicken, 1 (about 3½ pounds)

kosher salt and freshly ground pepper

peanut or grape seed oil, 1 tablespoon

unsalted butter, 4 tablespoons

large leeks, 2, white and pale green parts chopped

all-purpose flour, ¼ cup

hard apple cider, 1 bottle (12 ounces)

low-sodium chicken broth or stock, 1½ cups

fresh thyme, 1 teaspoon minced, plus sprigs for garnish

golden delicious apples, 2

fresh lemon juice, 1 tablespoon

applejack or calvados, ¼ cup

MAKES 4 SERVINGS

roasted chile-spiced chicken with pumpkin seed sauce

extra-virgin olive oil,
2 tablespoons, plus oil for the rack

whole chicken, 1 (about 4 pounds)

chili powder, 1 teaspoon

kosher salt and freshly ground pepper

garlic, 4 cloves, crushed, plus 1 clove, chopped

white onion, 1, chopped

jalapeño chile, 1, seeded and minced

diced tomatoes, 1 can (14½ ounces), drained

shelled pumpkin seeds, ⅓ cup, toasted (page 144)

fresh oregano, 1 tablespoon chopped

MAKES 4 SERVINGS

Preheat the oven to 425°F. Place a V-shaped roasting rack in a flameproof roasting pan and lightly oil the rack. Pull off any excess fat from around the chicken cavity and discard. Brush the chicken all over with 1 tablespoon of the oil. In a small bowl, mix the chili powder, 2 teaspoons salt, and ½ teaspoon pepper. Season the chicken inside and out with the chili powder mixture, then place the crushed garlic cloves in the cavity. Place the chicken on its side on the prepared rack in the pan. Roast for 20 minutes, then turn the chicken on its other side and roast for 20 minutes longer. Turn the chicken onto its back. Roast until golden brown and an instant-read thermometer inserted in the thickest part of the breast meat registers 170°F, 30–40 minutes longer.

In a medium frying pan over medium heat, heat the remaining 1 tablespoon oil. Add the onion and sauté until softened, about 3 minutes. Stir in the chopped garlic and jalapeño and cook until fragrant, about 1 minute longer. Stir in the tomatoes, pumpkin seeds, and oregano and cook just until the mixture is heated through, about 2 minutes. Transfer to a food processor and pulse until the pumpkin seeds are coarsely chopped.

When the chicken is ready, tilt the chicken so any juice in the cavity flows into the pan. Discard the crushed garlic. Transfer the chicken to a carving board and let rest for 10 minutes. Pour the pan juices into a glass measuring cup, let stand for about 2 minutes, then use a spoon to skim the fat from the surface. Return the pan juices to the roasting pan and place the pan on the stove top over medium heat. Add the tomato–pumpkin seed mixture and cook, scraping up the browned bits from the pan bottom, until hot, about 2 minutes. Taste and adjust the seasonings. Transfer the sauce to a warmed bowl or sauce boat.

Carve the chicken and serve right away. Pass the sauce at the table.

Shelled pumpkin seeds, also known as pepitas, give the chunky Mexican-inspired sauce paired with this chicken a rustic look. Toasting the seeds coaxes out their earthy, nutty taste, which is offset by the acidity of tomatoes, the heat of a jalapeño chile, and the herbal flavor of dried oregano.

cremini-stuffed chicken breasts with porcini pan sauce

Dried porcini mushrooms have a heady, intensely savory aroma. With such a concentrated earthy, meaty quality, porcinis deliver a huge flavor dividend. In this recipe, they combine with fresh cremini mushrooms to make a satisfying stuffing for chicken breasts, and their soaking liquid is the base for a light-bodied, but full-flavored, sauce.

Soak the porcini in the boiling water until softened, about 20 minutes. Lift out the porcini and coarsely chop. Pour the soaking liquid through a fine-mesh sieve lined with damp cheesecloth and set aside. In a food processor, combine the cremini and porcini mushrooms and pulse to finely chop. In a large frying pan over medium-high heat, melt the butter. Add the finely chopped mushrooms and sauté until they give off their juices and the juices evaporate, 8–10 minutes. During the last 2 minutes of cooking, stir in the shallot, 2 teaspoons of the parsley, and 1 teaspoon of the thyme. Season to taste with salt and pepper. Transfer to a bowl and let cool. Position a rack in the upper third of the oven and preheat to 425°F.

Season the chicken breasts with 1 teaspoon salt and ½ teaspoon pepper. Slip your fingers under the skin of each breast to loosen it, keeping the skin attached at one long side. Spoon one-fourth of the mushroom mixture under the skin of each breast and spread it evenly with your fingers. Place the stuffed breasts, skin side up, in a roasting pan and brush with the olive oil. Roast until golden brown and an instant-read thermometer inserted in the thickest part of the breast meat registers 170°F, 30–35 minutes. Transfer the breasts to a carving board and tent with aluminum foil to keep warm.

Pour off the fat in the pan. Place the pan on the stove top over medium-high heat. Pour in the reserved mushroom liquid and the Madeira and bring to a boil, scraping up the browned bits from the pan bottom. Boil until reduced to about ⅔ cup. Stir the cornstarch mixture to recombine, then add to the pan and cook just until the sauce is lightly thickened, about 10 seconds. Remove from the heat, taste, and adjust the seasonings.

Cut each breast half across the grain into slices ½ inch thick and place on a warmed dinner plate. Spoon some of the sauce over each serving and sprinkle with the reserved parsley and thyme. Serve right away.

dried porcini mushrooms, 1 ounce (1 cup lightly packed), rinsed

boiling water, 1¼ cups

cremini mushrooms, ½ pound, coarsely chopped

unsalted butter, 2 tablespoons

shallot, 1, minced

fresh flat-leaf parsley, 3 teaspoons chopped

fresh thyme, 1½ teaspoons minced

kosher salt and freshly ground pepper

boneless, skin-on chicken breast halves, 4 (about 10 ounces each)

extra-virgin olive oil, 1 tablespoon

madeira or dry marsala, 2 tablespoons

cornstarch, ½ teaspoon, mixed with 1 tablespoon cold water

MAKES 4 SERVINGS

Tart green tomatillos lend brightness to a southwestern poultry stew, which is further enlivened by other Mexican-style ingredients and earthy spices. Browning the turkey well is the first step to a deeply flavored dish.

turkey chile verde

Anaheim chiles have only a mild spiciness. They are renown for their meaty flesh and a green, vegetal flavor. Here, they add their character to this spin on green chile, a classic braise of Tex-Mex cooking, that marries the chiles with charred garlic and onions, tangy fresh tomatillos, and the minty, citrusy hints of cilantro.

Position an oven or broiler rack about 6 inches from the heat source and preheat the broiler. Place the tomatillos, onions, chiles, and garlic on a rimmed baking sheet and place under the broiler. Broil the vegetables, turning them occasionally and transferring them to a plate as they are ready. Remove the garlic when the skins are browned and the onion when the edges are browned, 5–6 minutes. Remove the chiles when charred and the tomatillos when charred but not split, about 8 minutes.

When the vegetables are cool enough to handle, remove and discard the skins from the garlic and chiles, and then discard the chile seeds and ribs. Discard the onion peels and coarsely chop the onions. Working in batches, combine the tomatillos, chiles, onions, garlic, cilantro, cumin, and oregano in a blender and process until smooth.

Skin the turkey thighs. Cut the meat off the bone, then cut the meat into 1½-inch chunks. Season with 2 teaspoons salt and ½ teaspoon pepper. In a large Dutch oven or other heavy pot with a lid, heat 2 tablespoons of the oil over medium-high heat. Working in batches, add the turkey and cook, stirring occasionally, until lightly browned, about 6 minutes per batch. Using a slotted spoon, transfer to a plate. Add the remaining 2 tablespoons oil to the pot. Pour in the tomatillo mixture and broth and bring to a boil, scraping up the browned bits from the pan bottom. Return the turkey to the pot, bring to a simmer, and then reduce the heat to medium-low, cover, and cook for 45 minutes.

After the turkey has cooked for 45 minutes, add the potatoes and continue to cook, covered, until the potatoes are tender, about 30 minutes longer. Taste and adjust the seasonings.

Ladle the chile into warmed deep bowls and serve right away.

tomatillos, 1½ pounds, husked, rinsed, and dried

white onions, 2, each cut into 8 wedges

anaheim chiles, 2

garlic, 5 large cloves, unpeeled

fresh cilantro leaves, 1 cup packed

ground cumin, 2 tablespoons

dried oregano, 2 tablespoons

bone-in, skin-on turkey thighs, 4 pounds

kosher salt and freshly ground pepper

extra-virgin olive oil, 4 tablespoons

low-sodium chicken broth or stock, 1 cup

red potatoes, 1½ pounds, cut into 1-inch chunks

MAKES 6 SERVINGS

indian-spiced grilled chicken legs with raita

lemons, 2

bone-in, skin-on whole chicken legs, 4 (about ¾ pound each)

kosher salt

garlic, 2 cloves

yellow onion, 1 small, chopped

plain yogurt, 2 cups

curry powder, 1 tablespoon

sweet paprika, 1 teaspoon

ground cinnamon, ¼ teaspoon

cayenne pepper, ⅛ teaspoon

canola oil for grilling

cucumber, 1, peeled, seeded, and coarsely grated

fresh mint, 1 tablespoon chopped, plus leaves for garnish

freshly ground pepper

MAKES 4 SERVINGS

Squeeze 2 tablespoons juice from 1 of the lemons. Cut the remaining lemon into 8 wedges and set aside to serve with the chicken.

Place the chicken in a large nonreactive baking dish and sprinkle evenly with the lemon juice and ¾ teaspoon salt. Cover and refrigerate for 1 hour.

Turn on a food processor and drop the garlic cloves through the feed tube to chop them. Stop the motor, add the onion, and pulse until puréed. Add 1 cup of the yogurt, the curry powder, paprika, cinnamon, and cayenne and pulse to combine. Pour the marinade over the chicken and mix well. Cover and refrigerate for at least 4 hours and up to 12 hours.

Prepare a charcoal or gas grill for indirect-heat cooking over high heat (page 143 or 144). Replace the grill grate and lightly oil it.

Lift each chicken leg from the yogurt mixture and shake gently to remove the excess marinade. Place the chicken, skin side down, on the cool side of the grill. Cover the grill and cook, without disturbing, until an instant-read thermometer inserted in the thickest part of the thigh meat registers 170°F (77°C), 30–35 minutes.

Meanwhile, to make the *raita,* in a small bowl, mix the remaining 1 cup yogurt, the cucumber, and chopped mint until blended. Season to taste with salt and pepper. Cover and refrigerate until ready to serve.

When the chicken is ready, transfer to a warmed platter and let rest for 5 minutes. Sprinkle with mint leaves. Serve right away. Pass the raita and lemon wedges at the table.

Curry powder gets its complexity of flavor from a blend of bold, fragrant spices; ground turmeric is the source of the powder's golden hue. Here, curry powder seasons a yogurt-based marinade that ensures the chicken stays tender and moist. The heat of a grill intensifies the spicy flavors and adds smokiness to the dish. Raita served alongside brings cool refreshment.

Woodsy fresh sage is the perfect counterpoint to a plump whole chicken that is slow-cooked on a smoky grill. The apples, too, are grilled and then tossed with sage and butter to help connect the flavor of the fruit to that of the bird.

cider-brined grill-roasted chicken with grilled apples and sage

hard apple cider, 1 bottle (12 ounces)

table salt, ½ cup

fresh sage, 2 tablespoons plus 2 teaspoons chopped

fresh rosemary, 2 tablespoons chopped

peppercorns, 1 teaspoon

bay leaf, 1

ice water, 6½ cups

whole chicken, 1 (about 4 pounds)

apple-wood or hickory chips, 1 cup

canola oil, 2 teaspoons, plus oil for grilling

golden delicious apples, 2

unsalted butter, 1 tablespoon, at room temperature

kosher salt and freshly ground pepper

MAKES 4 SERVINGS

In a small nonreactive saucepan over medium heat, combine the cider, table salt, the 2 tablespoons of chopped sage, the rosemary, peppercorns, and bay leaf and bring to a boil, stirring to dissolve the salt. Pour into a large, deep nonreactive bowl and let cool slightly. Stir in the ice water. Add the chicken, submerging it fully. Cover the chicken and refrigerate for at least 4 hours and up to 6 hours.

In a bowl, soak the wood chips in cold water to cover for at least 30 minutes and up to 2 hours. Drain the wood chips.

Prepare a charcoal or gas grill for indirect-heat cooking over high heat (page 143 or 144). Sprinkle the drained wood chips over the coals or use a wood-chip smoker box on the gas grill. Replace the grill grate and lightly oil it.

Remove the chicken from the brine; discard the brine. Place the chicken, breast side up, on the cool side of the grill. Cover the grill and cook the chicken until an instant-read thermometer inserted in the thickest part of the breast meat registers 170°F, about 1¼ hours. Transfer the chicken to a warmed platter and let rest for 10 minutes.

Peel and core the apples, and quarter each apple lengthwise. In a bowl, toss the apples with the 2 teaspoons oil to coat. Place the apples over the hot side of the grill and cook, turning occasionally, until seared with grill marks on all sides and tender-crisp, about 5 minutes. Transfer to a warmed serving bowl. Add the 2 teaspoons chopped sage to the apples, along with the butter, and toss to coat. Season to taste with kosher salt and pepper.

Arrange the apples on the platter around the chicken. Carve the chicken and serve right away.

Wood chips, soaked and scattered over a fire (or put in a smoker box on a gas grill), create woodsy, fragrant smoke that permeates a chicken as it cooks, flavoring every inch of the meat. Here, the chicken is first placed in a cider-and-herb brine before grilling. The result is a deeply seasoned, moist and tender bird with an irresistible smokiness.

winter

smoky roasted chicken breasts with potatoes and sherry sauce

extra-virgin olive oil, 4 tablespoons, plus oil for the pan

cumin seeds, 1 teaspoon

spanish smoked paprika, 2 teaspoons

dried oregano, 1 teaspoon

kosher salt and freshly ground pepper

bone-in, skin-on chicken breast halves, 4 (about ¾ pound each)

small yukon gold potatoes, 1½ pounds

garlic, 2 cloves, thinly sliced

dry sherry, ¼ cup

low-sodium chicken broth or stock, ½ cup

MAKES 4 SERVINGS

Preheat the oven to 425°F. Lightly oil a flameproof roasting pan.

Toast the cumin seeds (page 144) and pour onto a plate to cool. Using a mortar and pestle or a spice grinder, finely grind the cumin. In a small bowl, stir together the cumin, paprika, oregano, 2 teaspoons salt, and ½ teaspoon pepper.

Arrange the chicken breast halves, skin side up, in the prepared roasting pan. Brush the breasts with 1 tablespoon of the oil, and then season with the cumin mixture. Cut the unpeeled potatoes into quarters and place in a bowl. Add 2 tablespoons of the oil, 1 teaspoon salt, and ½ teaspoon pepper and toss to coat evenly. Scatter the potatoes around the breasts.

Roast, using a metal spatula to turn the potatoes occasionally, until an instant-read thermometer inserted in the thickest part of the breast meat registers 170°F, about 40 minutes. Transfer the chicken and potatoes to a warmed platter and tent with aluminum foil to keep warm.

Pour off the fat from the roasting pan. Place the pan on the stove top over medium heat. Add the remaining 1 tablespoon oil and the garlic and sauté until the garlic has softened but not browned, about 1 minute. Stir in the sherry and broth and bring to a boil, scraping up the browned bits from the pan bottom. Reduce the heat to medium and cook until reduced by half, about 3 minutes.

Pour the sauce over the chicken and potatoes and serve right away.

Spanish smoked paprika, known as pimentón, *is brick red in color and boasts a smoky flavor that is deliciously meaty, with earthy hints of cocoa. Its bold taste pairs well with the sharp-flavored cumin and aromatic oregano in the spice rub, and with the toasty garlic and nutty, crisp, dry sherry in the pan sauce.*

chicken pot pies with root vegetables and thyme crust

Butter plays a big role in these individual pot pies. A few tablespoons enrich the filling, giving it a round, full flavor that highlights the sweetness of the root vegetables. On top, the butter in the puff pastry adds opulent flavor to the crisp, golden crust that crowns the filling.

Peel the carrot and parsnip. Cut the carrot, parsnip, and unpeeled potato into ½-inch dice. Season the chicken with 1 teaspoon salt and ½ teaspoon pepper. In a Dutch oven or other heavy pot with a lid, heat the oil over medium-high heat until very hot but not smoking. Working in batches, add the chicken and cook, stirring occasionally, until lightly browned, about 5 minutes per batch. Using a slotted spoon, transfer to a plate.

Add the butter to the pot, reduce the heat to medium, and let the butter melt. Add the carrot, parsnip, potato, and ¼ cup water, reduce the heat to low, and cook the vegetables, stirring occasionally, until they begin to soften, about 5 minutes. Stir in the shallots and cook until softened, about 2 minutes. Meanwhile, fill a large bowl with ice water.

When the vegetables are ready, sprinkle the flour over them and stir well. Stir in the wine, broth, and 1 teaspoon of the thyme. Return the chicken to the pot, raise the heat to medium-high, and bring to a simmer, stirring often. Taste and adjust the seasonings. Transfer to a heatproof bowl and nest the bowl in the ice bath. Let stand, stirring occasionally, until tepid, about 30 minutes.

Preheat the oven to 375°F. Have ready four 4-cup ramekins, each about 4 inches in diameter. On a lightly floured work surface, roll out the puff pastry into a 12-inch square. Cut out four 4-inch squares. In a small bowl, beat the egg with a pinch of salt. Lightly brush the rim of each ramekin with the beaten egg. Divide the filling evenly among the ramekins. Top each ramekin with a pastry square, pressing it firmly around the rim. Place the ramekins on a rimmed baking sheet and refrigerate for 15 minutes.

Brush the pastry with the beaten egg and sprinkle with the remaining 1 teaspoon thyme. Bake until golden, 30–35 minutes. Serve right away.

carrot, 1 large

parsnip, 1 large

red potato, 1 large

boneless, skinless chicken thighs, 4, cut into 1-inch cubes

kosher salt and freshly ground pepper

peanut or grape seed oil, 2 tablespoons

unsalted butter, 3 tablespoons

shallots, 2, minced

all-purpose flour, ¼ cup, plus flour for rolling

dry white wine or dry vermouth, ½ cup

low-sodium chicken broth or stock, 2½ cups

fresh thyme, 2 teaspoons minced

frozen all-butter puff pastry, 1 sheet (about ½ pound), thawed

large egg, 1

MAKES 4 SERVINGS

A modern take on classic *coq au vin* uses slightly sweet Riesling instead of dry red wine as the braising liquid for a plump bird. Choose red pearl onions, if you can find them, to add color. A smoky high-quality bacon will help offset the fruitiness of the wine.

chicken braised with bacon, onions, and riesling

In this twist on a classic French recipe, Riesling is the foundation for the flavorful braising liquid, lending its fruitiness and subtle floral hints to the dish. A measure of Cognac fortifies the sauce and bacon adds a layer of smokiness. Small onions and carrots lend their aromatic qualities to help balance all the flavors.

Bring a saucepan of lightly salted water to a boil over high heat. Add the onions and cook until the skins loosen, about 2 minutes. Drain the onions and rinse under cold running water. Slip off and discard the skins. Cut the chicken into 9 pieces (page 142), then season with 1½ teaspoons salt and ½ teaspoon pepper.

In a Dutch oven or other heavy pot with a lid, fry the bacon over medium heat until crisp and browned, about 8 minutes. Transfer the bacon to paper towels to drain, leaving the fat in the pot.

Raise the heat under the pot to medium-high. Working in batches, add the chicken, skin side down, and cook, turning once or twice, until lightly browned on both sides, about 5 minutes per batch. Transfer to a platter. Add the onions and carrots to the pot and cook, stirring occasionally, until lightly browned, about 3 minutes. Add the shallots and cook, stirring occasionally, until softened, about 1 minute. Carefully add the Cognac and reduce the heat to low. Using a long-handled match, light the Cognac and let the flame burn for 30 seconds, then cover to extinguish the flame. Uncover, add the Riesling, and bring to a boil over high heat. Return the drumsticks, thighs, and wings, then the breasts, to the pot. Reduce the heat to medium-low, cover, and simmer for 35 minutes.

In a heatproof bowl, mash together the butter and flour to form a thick paste. Gradually whisk about 1 cup of the hot cooking liquid into the flour-butter mixture, and then stir this mixture into the pot. Simmer until the chicken shows no sign of pink when pierced with the tip of a sharp knife near the bone, 5–10 minutes longer. Taste and adjust the seasonings. Crumble the bacon and sprinkle the bacon and thyme over the chicken.

Transfer the chicken to a warmed deep platter. Serve right away.

red or white boiling onions, 12

whole chicken, 1 (about 4 pounds)

kosher salt and freshly ground pepper

thick-cut bacon, 4 slices

small carrots, 12

shallots, 2, minced

cognac or other brandy, 2 tablespoons

riesling, 2 cups

unsalted butter, 3 tablespoons, at room temperature

all-purpose flour, 3 tablespoons

fresh thyme, 1½ teaspoons chopped

MAKES 4 SERVINGS

sautéed chicken breasts with bitter orange sauce

navel oranges, 2 large

boneless, skinless chicken breast halves, 4 (about 6 ounces each)

kosher salt and freshly ground pepper

peanut or grape seed oil, 2 tablespoons

unsalted butter, 1 tablespoon

shallot, 1, minced

orange-flavored liqueur, 2 tablespoons

bitter orange marmalade, ½ cup

low-sodium chicken broth or stock, ⅓ cup

balsamic vinegar, 1 tablespoon

MAKES 4 SERVINGS

Using a vegetable peeler, remove the zest from 1 orange in strips. Using a chef's knife, cut the strips into very thin shreds and set aside. Cut a slice off of the top and bottom of the orange. Stand the orange upright and, following the contour of fruit, slice off the remaining peel and pith. Working over a bowl, cut along both sides of each segment to free it from the membrane; let the segments and juice fall into the bowl. Squeeze the juice from the membrane into the bowl. Repeat with the second orange, omitting the removal of the zest.

Using a flat meat pounder, pound each chicken breast half until flattened to an even thickness of about ¾ inch. Season the chicken breasts with 1 teaspoon salt and ½ teaspoon pepper.

In a large frying pan over medium-high heat, heat the oil until very hot but not smoking. Add the chicken breasts and reduce the heat to medium. Cook until golden brown, 4–5 minutes. Turn the breasts over and cook until the second sides are browned and the chicken springs back when pressed in the center, about 4 minutes longer. Transfer to a plate.

Reduce the heat to low, add the butter to the pan, and allow it to melt. Add the shallot and sauté until softened, about 2 minutes. Remove from the heat and add the liqueur. Using a long-handled match, light the liqueur and let the flame burn for 30 seconds, then cover the pan to extinguish the flame. Uncover, return the pan to medium-high heat, and stir in the marmalade, broth, and vinegar. Simmer the sauce, stirring occasionally, about 2 minutes. During the last 30 seconds, add the orange segments and juice and heat through. Taste and adjust the seasonings.

Transfer the chicken to a warmed platter. Spoon the sauce and orange segments over the top and garnish with the zest shreds. Serve right away.

Here, orange marmalade is the base for a simple glaze-like sauce. It offers its sweet, yet pleasingly bitter, orange flavor and adds texture and body. Oranges are layered into the dish in a few other guises—sweet segments and juice, fiery liqueur, and aromatic zest—with each element contributing to the heady citrus essence.

Coriander and cumin seeds, toasted to bring out their flavors, are a savory foil to salty-sour preserved lemons in an aromatic, Moroccan-style braise. Together they lend an exotic flair to a warming chicken dish, perfect for a cold winter evening.

braised chicken with quick-preserved meyer lemons

meyer lemons, 2

kosher salt and freshly ground pepper

coriander seeds and cumin seeds, 1½ teaspoons *each*

sweet paprika and ground ginger, 1 teaspoon *each*

ground cinnamon, ½ teaspoon

cayenne pepper, ¼ teaspoon

whole chicken, 1 (about 4 pounds)

extra-virgin olive oil, 2 tablespoons

yellow onion, 1, chopped

garlic, 2 cloves, minced

diced tomatoes, 1 can (28 ounces), drained

low-sodium chicken broth or stock, 1 cup

chickpeas, 1 can (15 ounces), rinsed and drained

fresh cilantro, 1 tablespoon coarsely chopped

MAKES 4 SERVINGS

Slice the lemons into rounds about ⅛ inch thick, discarding any seeds. Sprinkle 1 tablespoon salt on a plate and arrange the lemon slices on the salt. Sprinkle the slices with another 1 tablespoon salt. Let stand while preparing the chicken.

Toast the coriander and cumin seeds together (see page 144) and pour onto a plate to cool. Using a mortar and pestle or a spice grinder, finely grind the coriander and cumin. Transfer to a small bowl and stir in the paprika, ginger, cinnamon, and cayenne. Cut the chicken into 9 pieces (page 142), then season with 1½ teaspoons salt and ½ teaspoon pepper.

In a Dutch oven or other heavy pot with a lid, heat the oil over medium-high heat until very hot but not smoking. Working in batches, add the chicken, skin side down, and cook, turning once or twice, until deeply browned on both sides, about 10 minutes per batch. Transfer to a platter.

Add the onion and sauté until golden, about 6 minutes. Add the garlic and sauté until fragrant, about 1 minute. Add the spice mixture and stir for 15 seconds. Stir in the drained tomatoes and broth and bring to a boil, scraping up the browned bits from the pan bottom. Return the drumsticks, thighs, and wings, then the breasts, to the pot. Reduce the heat to medium-low, cover, and simmer for 40 minutes. Meanwhile, rinse and drain the lemon slices and finely dice them.

Stir the diced lemon and chickpeas into the pot and continue to cook until the chicken shows no sign of pink when pierced with the tip of a sharp knife near the bone, 5–10 minutes longer.

Remove the pot from the heat and let stand for 5 minutes. Skim off any fat that rises to the top of the cooking liquid. Transfer the chicken to a warmed deep platter and sprinkle with the cilantro. Serve right away.

Mildly tart Meyer lemons have a full, ripe, almost floral aroma. This recipe includes a method for making an easy version of Moroccan preserved lemons that very quickly draws out bold flavor from thin slices of Meyer lemons. Their citrusy intensity adds sunny notes to this braised dish that is fragrant with spices.

breaded chicken cutlets with green olive–lemon relish

Plump, fleshy green olives have a salty, meaty, well-rounded flavor and hints of fruitiness. They are the backbone of this rustic Mediterranean-inspired relish. Tangy lemon juice and zest, briny capers, fresh parsley, and fruity olive oil each add their character to this savory accompaniment for crisp breaded chicken breasts.

To make the relish, finely grate the zest from the lemon, and then squeeze 2 tablespoons lemon juice. Turn on a food processor and drop the garlic through the feed tube to chop it. Stop the motor, add the olives, capers, parsley, anchovy paste, pepper flakes, and lemon zest and juice, and pulse to coarsely chop the olives. With the machine running, add ½ cup of the oil in a slow, steady stream and process until olives are roughly chopped or according to your preference. Transfer to a serving bowl. Cover and let stand to blend the flavors while preparing the chicken.

Using a flat meat pounder, pound each chicken breast half until flattened to an even thickness of about ½ inch.

Line a baking sheet with parchment or waxed paper. In a shallow dish, stir together the flour, ½ teaspoon salt, and ½ teaspoon pepper. In a bowl, whisk together the eggs and the 1 tablespoon oil. In a second shallow bowl, stir together the bread crumbs, oregano, and basil. One breast half at a time, dip the chicken in the flour mixture, coating evenly and shaking off the excess. Then dip in the egg mixture, coating evenly and allowing the excess to drip off. Finally, coat evenly with the bread crumb mixture. Transfer to the prepared baking sheet. Let stand for 5 minutes.

Line another baking sheet with paper towels. In a very large frying pan over medium heat, heat the remaining ¼ cup oil until very hot but not smoking. Add the chicken breasts and cook, adjusting the heat as needed, until golden brown, about 4 minutes. Turn and cook until the second sides are browned, 3–4 minutes longer. Using a slotted spatula, transfer the chicken to the paper towels to drain briefly, no longer than 30 seconds.

Transfer the chicken to a warmed platter and top each breast with a spoonful of the relish. Serve right away.

lemon, 1

garlic, 1 clove

pitted green olives, 2 cups (10 ounces)

nonpareil capers, 3 tablespoons

fresh flat-leaf parsley, 3 tablespoons chopped

anchovy paste, 1 teaspoon

red pepper flakes, ¼ teaspoon

extra-virgin olive oil, ¾ cup plus 1 tablespoon

boneless, skinless chicken breast halves, 4 (about 6 ounces each)

all-purpose flour, ½ cup

kosher salt and freshly ground pepper

large eggs, 2

panko bread crumbs, 1 cup

dried oregano, 1 teaspoon

dried basil, 1 teaspoon

MAKES 4 SERVINGS

chicken wings in fermented black bean sauce

fermented black beans,
1 tablespoon

green onion, 1

**low-sodium chicken broth
or stock,** ½ cup

soy sauce, 2 tablespoons

**chinese rice wine or dry
sherry,** 2 tablespoons

**chinese chile sauce with
garlic,** 1 tablespoon

sugar, 1 tablespoon

oyster sauce, 2 teaspoons

chicken wings, 3 pounds

peanut or grape seed oil,
3 tablespoons

fresh ginger, one ½-inch
piece, peeled and minced

garlic, 3 cloves, minced

asian sesame oil for serving

MAKES 4 SERVINGS

Place the beans in a fine-mesh sieve and rinse under cold running water. Drain well, and then chop coarsely.

Finely chop the white and pale green bottom of the green onion and set aside. Thinly slice the green onion top and set aside separately. In a small bowl, stir together the broth, soy sauce, rice wine, chile sauce, sugar, and oyster sauce to dissolve the sugar.

Cut off and discard the tips of the chicken wings (or reserve for making stock). Heat a very large frying pan over medium-high heat until very hot. Add 2 tablespoons of the oil and swirl the pan to coat it well. Add the chicken wings and cook, turning occasionally, until browned on both sides, about 5 minutes. Transfer the wings to a platter.

Add the remaining 1 tablespoon oil to the frying pan over medium-high heat. Add the green onion bottom, ginger, and garlic and stir until the garlic is fragrant, about 15 seconds. Stir in the broth mixture and the black beans. Return the chicken wings to the pan and reduce the heat to medium-low. Cover and simmer until the chicken shows no sign of pink when pierced with the tip of a sharp knife near the bone, about 30 minutes.

Uncover and raise the heat to high. Boil, stirring often, until the liquid is reduced to a glaze, about 3 minutes.

Transfer the wings and their sauce to a warmed serving platter. Sprinkle with the green onion top, drizzle with sesame oil, and serve right away.

An array of Chinese-style condiments and flavoring pastes combine in this recipe to create a simple sauce for braised chicken wings with layers of complex flavor. Sweet, salty, tart, and spicy at the same time, this dish offers an exotic twist on chicken wings for your next casual party.

To satisfy a salad craving during the cooler months of the year, choose sturdy winter greens and bolster them with cubes of toasted country bread. The bread cubes soak up the flavorful juices of a roast chicken when served alongside.

roasted chicken with warm winter greens salad

whole chicken, 1 (about 4 pounds)

crusty country bread, 2 slices, ¾ inch thick, cut into cubes

extra-virgin olive oil, 2 tablespoons, plus oil for the rack

kosher salt and freshly ground pepper

shallot, 1, minced

garlic, 1 clove, minced

low-sodium chicken broth or stock, ½ cup

sherry vinegar, 2 tablespoons

walnut oil, 2 tablespoons

mixed winter salad greens such as frisée, radicchio, escarole, and chicory, 6–8 cups

walnuts, ½ cup, toasted (page 144) and coarsely chopped

dried cranberries, ½ cup

MAKES 4 SERVINGS

Pull off the fat from around the chicken's cavity and coarsely chop the fat. In a small saucepan over low heat, cook the fat until rendered, about 15 minutes. Strain through a fine-mesh sieve; you should have about 1½ tablespoons fat. Let the chicken and fat stand at room temperature for 1–2 hours. Preheat the oven to 350°F. Place the bread cubes in a bowl, drizzle with the oil and toss, then spread on a rimmed baking sheet. Toast in the oven, stirring occasionally, until golden, about 15 minutes. Let cool.

Raise the oven temperature to 425°F. Place a V-shaped roasting rack in a flameproof roasting pan and lightly oil the rack. Rub the rendered fat all over the exterior of the chicken and season the chicken inside and out with 2 teaspoons salt and ½ teaspoon pepper. Place the chicken on its side on the rack in the pan. Roast for 20 minutes. Turn the chicken on its other side and roast for 20 minutes longer. Turn the chicken on its back and roast until golden brown and an instant-read thermometer inserted in the thickest part of the breast meat registers 170°F, about 40 minutes. Tilt the chicken so any juice in the cavity flows into the pan. Transfer the chicken to a carving board and let rest for 10 minutes.

Meanwhile, to make the vinaigrette, pour off all but 2 tablespoons of the drippings from the roasting pan. Place the pan on the stove top over medium heat. Add the shallot and garlic and cook, stirring often, until the shallot has softened, about 2 minutes. Stir in the broth, vinegar, and walnut oil. Bring to a boil over high heat, scraping up the browned bits from the pan bottom. Remove from the heat. Taste and adjust the seasonings.

In a large bowl, combine the salad greens, bread cubes, walnuts, and dried cranberries. Add the warm vinaigrette and toss to coat. Divide the salad among warmed dinner plates. Cut the chicken into quarters and place a chicken quarter on top of each salad. Serve right away.

In this recipe for simple, satisfying winter fare, sweet yet tangy dried cranberries dot a salad of pleasantly bitter greens. They add bright bursts of flavor that offset the buttery toasted walnuts in the salad, the warm vinaigrette made with pan drippings, and the richness of the golden brown roasted bird.

claypot caramel chicken with shiitake mushrooms and broccoli

This classic of Vietnamese cooking is unusual in its liberal use of sugar. The sugar is cooked into a deep-amber caramel that brings a sweet-and-savory bittersweetness as well as a rich reddish-brown hue to the sauce. Fish sauce, shallots, ginger, garlic, and chile create layers of delicious, enticing flavors.

In a bowl, soak the shiitake mushrooms in warm water to cover until softened, about 30 minutes. Drain and rinse under cold running water. Cut off and discard the tough stems, then cut each cap in half.

In a heavy-bottomed saucepan over medium-high heat, combine the sugar and 2 tablespoons water and cook, stirring constantly, until the sugar dissolves. Continue to cook without stirring, occasionally swirling the pan, until the mixture turns a deep copper-brown, about 3 minutes. Carefully stir in the broth and fish sauce. The caramel will solidify. Continue to cook, stirring constantly, until the caramel melts again. Remove from the heat.

In a flameproof clay pot or Dutch oven, heat 1 tablespoon of the oil over medium-high heat until very hot but not smoking. Working in batches, add the chicken thighs and cook, stirring occasionally, until lightly browned, about 5 minutes per batch. Using a slotted spoon, transfer to a plate.

When all of the chicken has been browned, add the remaining 1 tablespoon oil to the pot and heat until very hot but not smoking. Add the shallots, ginger, garlic, and chile and stir until fragrant, about 15 seconds. Return the chicken to the pot, stir in the caramel mixture, raise the heat to high, and bring to a boil. Reduce the heat to medium-low, cover, and simmer until the chicken shows no sign of pink when pierced with a sharp knife, about 30 minutes. During the last 5 minutes, add the shiitake mushrooms.

Bring a saucepan of lightly salted water to a boil over high heat. Add the broccoli and cook until tender-crisp, about 2 minutes. Drain in a colander. Just before serving, add the broccoli to the pot and stir to mix and heat through.

Spoon the chicken and vegetables into warmed bowls and serve right away.

dried shiitake mushrooms, 12

sugar, ½ cup

low-sodium chicken broth or stock, ¾ cup

asian fish sauce, 2 tablespoons

peanut or grape seed oil, 2 tablespoons

boneless, skinless chicken thighs, 5 (about 1¾ pounds total weight), cut into 1-inch pieces

shallots, 3, sliced crosswise into thin rings

fresh ginger, one 1-inch piece, peeled and minced

garlic, 3 cloves, minced

thai or serrano chile, 1, sliced into thin rings

kosher salt

broccoli florets, 2 cups

MAKES 4 SERVINGS

mexican lime soup with chicken

small limes, 8–10

bone-in, skin-on chicken breast halves, 2 (about 10 ounces each)

kosher salt and freshly ground pepper

extra-virgin olive oil, 1 tablespoon

white onion, 1 large, chopped

garlic, 5 cloves, minced

jalapeño chile, 1, seeded and minced

low-sodium chicken broth or stock, 3 cups

dried oregano, 1½ teaspoons

hass avocado, 1

queso fresco or ricotta salata cheese, 2 ounces

organic tortilla chips, 2 cups

MAKES 6 SERVINGS

Cut 2 limes into wedges, and set aside to serve with the soup. Juice as many of the remaining limes as needed to measure ¼ cup.

Season the chicken breast halves with 1 teaspoon salt and ½ teaspoon pepper. In a large saucepan over medium heat, warm the oil. Add the chicken, skin side down, and cook until browned, about 5 minutes; transfer the chicken to a plate. Add the onion to the pan and sauté until translucent, about 4 minutes. Stir in the garlic and chile and sauté until fragrant, about 1 minute. Stir in the broth, 3 cups water, the lime juice, and the oregano, and then return the chicken to the saucepan.

Raise the heat to high and bring the liquid to a boil, skimming off any foam that rises to the surface. Reduce the heat to medium-low, cover partially, and simmer until the chicken shows no sign of pink when pierced with the tip of a sharp knife near the bone, about 40 minutes.

Transfer the chicken to a carving board, keeping the soup at a simmer. Let the chicken cool slightly. Remove and discard the skin and bones, and shred the chicken into bite-sized pieces. Stir the chicken into the soup. Taste and adjust the seasonings.

Pit, peel, and dice the avocado and place in a small bowl. Crumble the cheese into another small bowl. Place the tortilla chips and lime wedges in separate bowls. Ladle the soup into warmed soup bowls and serve right away. Pass the avocado, cheese, tortilla chips, and lime wedges at the table.

This Mexican-inspired version of familiar chicken soup gets its zip from lots of puckery lime juice. Limes' uniquely bright, bracing sharpness is countered by fragrant garlic, herbal oregano, and spicy jalapeño. The garnishes not only add color and texture, but also depth and complexity to the vibrant soup.

Here, the distinctly flavored juice of winter tangerines enlivens braised chicken thighs, whose dark, rich meat contrasts beautifully with the tart fruit. Exotic star anise perfumes the dish with its unique fragrance to create a modern spin on a traditional Chinese recipe.

braised chicken with tangerine and star anise

Here, vibrant fresh tangerines, which are at their best in the winter, add a tart-sweet and exotic element to a star anise–infused braising liquid. Their fragrant juice and zest perk up the deep flavors in the dish and cut through the richness of the tender braised chicken thighs.

Finely grate the zest from the tangerines, then squeeze ½ cup tangerine juice. Pull off and discard the skin from the chicken thighs. Season the chicken with 1 teaspoon salt and ½ teaspoon pepper.

In a Dutch oven or other heavy pot with a lid, heat the oil over medium-high heat until very hot but not smoking. Working in batches, add the chicken and cook, turning once or twice, until browned on both sides, about 9 minutes per batch. Transfer to a plate.

Pour off all but 1 tablespoon of the fat from the pot and return the pot to medium heat. Add the onion and cook, stirring occasionally, until softened, 3–4 minutes. Add the garlic, ginger, and half of the tangerine zest and stir until fragrant, about 1 minute. Add the broth, tangerine juice, soy sauce, Sriracha sauce, and star anise and bring to a boil, scraping up the browned bits from the pot bottom. Return the chicken thighs to the pot, reduce the heat to low, cover, and simmer until the chicken shows no sign of pink when pierced with the tip of a sharp knife near the bone, about 25 minutes.

Transfer the chicken to a warmed platter. Remove and discard the star anise. Bring the liquid in the pot to a boil over medium-high heat. In a small bowl, mix the cornstarch and 1 tablespoon water. Stir the cornstarch mixture into the liquid in the pot and cook just until the sauce thickens slightly, about 30 seconds.

Pour the sauce over the chicken. Sprinkle with the remaining tangerine zest and serve right away.

tangerines, 2

bone-in, skin-on chicken thighs, 8 (about 3¼ pounds total weight)

kosher salt and freshly ground pepper

peanut oil, 2 tablespoons

yellow onion, 1 small, finely chopped

garlic, 2 cloves, minced

fresh ginger, one ¼-inch piece, peeled and minced

low-sodium chicken broth or stock, 1 cup

soy sauce, 2 tablespoons

sriracha sauce, 1 teaspoon

whole star anise, 2

cornstarch, 2 teaspoons

MAKES 4 SERVINGS

fundamentals

In this section, you will find essential information about working with chicken. From how to select the best bird at the market to how to carve it once it's cooked, along with helpful tips for preparing some of the frequently used ingredients in this book—— all the basics are covered here. You will also find recipes for key elements used in chicken dishes and a few recipes for simple side dishes to complete the meal.

choosing a chicken

There is often more than just one type of chicken in the refrigerator case. If you're unsure of the differences between the types, here is what you need to know.

organic Organic poultry is raised without antibiotics or growth hormones and is given organically grown feed. Note that in order to carry the "organic" label, foods, including poultry, must be certified, a process that costs time and money. Some small producers, therefore, do not to apply for certification even though their products may conform with organic standards.

free-range Poultry that is allowed access to the outdoors can be labeled free-range. Some say that the exercise and more varied diet of free-range birds translates to more flavorful and better-textured meat.

kosher Kosher birds are processed under rabbinical supervision. Their processing differs slightly from that of regular birds and is the reason why kosher birds often have a few feathers still attached (they should be pulled out before cooking). Kosher birds are treated with salt; though they are rinsed before packaging, the salt does penetrate into the meat. For this reason, if you are following a recipe that calls for brining, do not use a kosher bird—the finished dish may taste overseasoned.

handling raw poultry

All poultry is subject to contamination by harmful bacteria. Salmonella has been particularly linked with raw or undercooked chicken and turkey, but it is killed at about 160°F. Cold temperatures inhibit bacterial growth, so refrigerate poultry as soon as possible after purchase.

When cooking, always handle raw poultry carefully to avoid cross-contamination of food-preparation surfaces and utensils, and never allow it to come into contact with foods that will be eaten raw or only partially cooked. It is also a good idea to reserve one cutting board for raw poultry, meats, and seafood and another for produce, and to wash the boards thoroughly with hot, soapy water and dry well between uses.

cutting up a whole chicken

Cutting up a whole chicken takes some practice, but is a good skill to master.

1 Remove the legs Place the chicken, breast side up, on a cutting board. Pull a leg away from the body. Using poultry shears, cut through the skin to expose the hip joint. Cut through the joint to remove the leg. Repeat with the second leg.

2 Separate the thighs and drumsticks Locate the joint between the thigh and drumstick on a leg. Using the shears, cut through the joint to separate the thigh from the drumstick. Repeat with the second leg.

3 Remove the wings Grasp a wing and pull it away from the body. Use the shears to cut through the skin to expose the shoulder joint, then cut through the joint to remove the wing. Repeat with the second wing.

4 Remove the back On one side of the breast, locate the line of fat that runs from near the tip of the breast to the joint where the wing was attached. Use the shears to cut along this line. Repeat with the other side, separating the breast from the back.

5 Pull out the breastbone Turn the breast over and run the tip of the shears through the membrane covering the breastbone and cartilage. Bend the breast upward at the center to pop out the breastbone, then pull or cut it free and discard.

6 Cut the breast into halves Using the shears, cut the breast lengthwise into halves. You will have a total of 8 serving pieces plus the back, which can be reserved for making stock.

butterflying a chicken

Butterflying a chicken requires only two easy cuts. A sturdy pair of poultry shears is the best tool for the job.

1 Remove the backbone Place the chicken, breast side down, on a board. Using poultry shears, cut along one side, and then the other side, of the backbone, cutting it free. Discard the backbone or reserve it for making stock.

2 Flatten the chicken Turn the chicken breast side up, opening the cavity so that the chicken is lying flat. Using both hands, press firmly on the breast area to break the breastbone and completely flatten the bird. You should hear and feel the breastbone crack.

3 Tuck the wing tips Bend the wing tips to tuck them under the chicken, behind the area where the breast and wing are joined.

testing for doneness

Different types of poultry should be cooked to different degrees of doneness. Depending on the cut, doneness is gauged with an instant-read thermometer or by using tactile clues.

chicken To test a whole chicken or chicken parts for doneness, insert an instant-read thermometer into the thickest part of the meat—breast or thigh—without touching the bone, which can skew the reading. The internal temperature should reach 170°F.

Some cuts are too thin to test accurately with a thermometer. For a boneless chicken breast, the center should feel firm and spring back when pressed with a fingertip. Small chicken pieces that are stir-fried should be opaque throughout when cut into.

turkey Turkey breast should be cooked until the thickest part of the meat reaches 165°F on an instant-read thermometer.

duck Duck breasts are best eaten when still rosy in color. They should be cooked to an internal temperature of 135° to 140°F.

carving a whole chicken

Before carving, remember to allow the bird to rest. This helps the meat retain juices so that it is moist and flavorful.

1 Remove the legs Using a carving knife, cut through the skin between the breast and thigh. Gently pull the leg away from the body and locate the thigh joint and then cut through the joint to free the leg. Repeat with the second leg.

2 Separate the thighs Cut through the joint between the drumstick and thigh to separate them. Repeat with the second leg.

3 Remove the wings Cut through the skin between a wing and the breast. Locate the shoulder joint and cut through it to remove the wing. Repeat on the other side to remove the second wing.

4 Make a base cut at the breast Make a horizontal cut between the breast meat and the bone so that when carving, the slices will fall away easily. Repeat on the other side.

5 Carve the breasts Make a series of cuts into the breast, parallel with the center breastbone, carving the meat in long, thin slices. Repeat on the other side.

preparing a charcoal grill

A 22-inch round kettle grill is the best choice for the charcoal-grilled recipes in this book.

direct-heat grilling over medium-high heat Ignite about 2½ pounds of coals and let the coals burn until covered with a layer of white ash. Spread the coals in an even layer on the fire bed and then let the coals burn until medium-hot, 20–30 minutes.

indirect-heat grilling over high heat Ignite about 2½ pounds of coals and let them burn until covered with a layer of white ash. Arrange the coals in an even pile in one half of the fire bed, leaving the other half free of coals.

preparing a gas grill

Before using a propane gas–fueled grill, be sure that there is enough propane in the tank.

direct-heat grilling over medium-high heat Turn all the burners to high heat. Close the cover and preheat the grill for 10–20 minutes, then reduce the heat to medium-high.

indirect-heat grilling over high heat Turn all the burners to high heat. Close the cover and preheat the grill for 10–20 minutes. Turn off all but 1 of the burners. (If using a wood-chip smoker box, follow the manufacturer's directions for filling the box and igniting the wood chips.)

working with herbs

The different leaf shapes and textures of herbs require different methods of preparation. Here is how to work with the herbs commonly used in the book.

chopping parsley, mint, cilantro, sage, or tarragon Pull off the leaves from the stems. Gather the leaves on a cutting board and then rock a chef's knife back and forth over the leaves until chopped into large pieces (coarsely chop). Regather the leaves and rock the blade over them until chopped into pieces as small as possible (mince).

chopping thyme and rosemary Gently run your thumb and index finger down the stems to remove the leaves. Gather the leaves on a cutting board. Rock a chef's knife back and forth over the leaves to chop into large pieces (coarsely chop). Regather the leaves and rock the blade over them until they are chopped into pieces as small as possible (mince).

snipping chives Gather the chives into a small bundle and place on a cutting board. Using a very sharp chef's knife, cut the chives crosswise into small pieces. Chives can also be snipped with kitchen shears.

toasting nuts, seeds, and spices

Toasting coaxes out flavor. For the best results, allow toasted nuts, seeds, and spices to cool completely before use.

nuts Spread the nuts in an even layer on a baking sheet and toast in a 350°F oven until lightly browned and fragrant, about 10 minutes, stirring occasionally.

seeds, spices, and pine nuts Place the item in a small, dry skillet and set the skillet over medium heat. Toast, stirring occasionally, until fragrant and slightly darkened in color, 2–5 minutes, depending on the size and quantity of the seeds, spices, or nuts.

chicken stock

4 sprigs fresh flat-leaf parsley

1 sprig fresh thyme

1 dried bay leaf

8 whole peppercorns

5 pounds chicken backs or wings, or a combination, chopped into 2- to 3-inch pieces

2 tablespoons canola oil

1 large yellow onion, coarsely chopped

1 large carrot, coarsely chopped

1 large stalk celery with leaves, coarsely chopped

Wrap the parsley, thyme, bay leaf, and peppercorns in a piece of damp cheesecloth and secure with kitchen string; set aside.

Position an oven rack in the upper third of the oven and preheat to 425°F. Spread the chicken parts in a large roasting pan. Roast for 30 minutes. Turn the pieces over and continue roasting until deeply browned, about 20 minutes longer.

In a stockpot over medium-high heat, warm the oil. When hot, add the onion, carrot, and celery and cook, stirring occasionally, until they start to brown, 10–12 minutes.

Using tongs, transfer the browned chicken to the stockpot. Pour off and discard any fat in the roasting pan. Place the roasting pan over 2 burners on high heat and warm until the juices sizzle. Pour 2 cups water into the roasting pan. Bring to a boil, scraping up the browned bits with a wooden spoon. Pour the liquid from the roasting pan into the stockpot and add the herb bundle. Add water to cover the ingredients by about 1 inch.

Turn the heat to high and bring the liquid almost to a boil.

As soon as bubbles form, reduce the heat to low. Skim off any foam from the surface and discard. Let the stock simmer, skimming any foam from the surface, for at least 3 hours and up to 6 hours. Add additional water, if necessary, to keep the ingredients just covered. Do not let the stock boil.

Line a large fine-mesh sieve with damp cheesecloth and place over a large heatproof bowl. Pour the stock through the sieve and discard the solids. Let the stock stand for 5 minutes, then carefully skim the clear yellow fat from the surface.

Let the stock cool to room temperature, then cover and refrigerate for up to 3 days. Or, pour into airtight containers and freeze for up to 3 months. Makes about 3 quarts.

truffle butter

1 black or white truffle (about ½ ounce)

6 tablepoons unsalted butter, at room temperature

Using a truffle shaver or very sharp, thin-bladed knife, shave the truffle into very thin slices. Coarsely chop the truffle shavings. Transfer to a bowl, add the butter, and mix with a rubber spatula until well combined.

Cover and let stand at room temperature for 4 hours to infuse the butter with the truffle flavor. Makes about ½ cup.

crème fraîche

1 cup heavy cream

1 tablespoon buttermilk

In a small saucepan over medium-low heat, combine the cream and buttermilk. Heat just until the mixture is lukewarm (do not allow the mixture to simmer). Transfer the mixture to a nonreactive bowl, cover, and let stand at warm room temperature until thickened, at least 8 hours and up to 48 hours. Refrigerate until well chilled before using. Makes 1 cup.

mashed potatoes

2½ pounds russet potatoes, peeled and cut into 2-inch chunks

1½ teaspoons salt

6 tablespoons unsalted butter

½ cup half-and-half, warmed

⅛ teaspoon freshly ground white pepper

Put the potatoes in a large saucepan and add water to cover by 1 inch. Add 1 teaspoon of the salt. Place the pan over high heat and bring the water to a boil, then reduce the heat to a simmer. Cover and simmer the potatoes until tender when pierced with the tip of a paring knife, 15–18 minutes.

Drain the potatoes and return them to the pan. For a chunky texture, mash the potatoes with a potato masher; for a smooth texture, pass the potatoes through a ricer back into the pan. Place the pan over low heat. Stir

in the butter, followed by the half-and-half, a little at a time. Mix in the remaining ½ teaspoon salt and the pepper. Serve right away. Makes 4–6 servings.

steamed fragrant rice

1 cup jasmine or basmati rice

1½ cups water

Place the rice in a fine-mesh sieve and rinse under cold running water until the water runs clear. Transfer the rice to a heavy saucepan and add the water. Cover the pan, place it over high heat, and bring to a boil. Reduce the heat to low and simmer, undisturbed, for about 20 minutes. Remove from the heat and let stand, covered, for 5 minutes. Fluff the rice with a fork and serve right away. Makes 4–6 servings.

polenta

5 cups water

1½ cups fine-ground polenta

½ teaspoon salt

In a large saucepan over medium-high heat, bring the water to a boil. Whisking constantly, add the polenta in a slow stream. Stir in the salt, reduce the heat to medium-low, and continue to cook, stirring constantly, until the polenta thickens and pulls away from the sides of the pan, about 20 minutes. Serve right away. Makes 4–6 servings.

seasonal ingredients

All fruits and vegetables have a season when they are at their best. The chart at right indicates the seasonality of most of the types of produce used in this book. Note that though some fruits and vegetables, such as apples and eggplants, are available thoughout the year, they do have seasons when they are at their peak. Solid dots indicate peak seasons; open dots indicate transitional seasons.

INGREDIENTS	SPRING	SUMMER	FALL	WINTER
apples			●	○
arugula	●	●	●	
asparagus	●			
avocados	●	●	●	●
bell peppers, red		●	●	
celery root			●	○
cherries, bing		●		
chicory	○			●
chiles, fresh		●	●	
corn		●		
cranberries			●	· ○
eggplants, asian		●	○	
escarole			●	●
fava beans	●			
fennel	●	●	●	●
frisée			●	●
green garlic	●			
key limes	●	●		
leeks	●	○	●	●
lemongrass	●	●	●	●
lettuces	●	●	●	●

INGREDIENTS	SPRING	SUMMER	FALL	WINTER
limes	○			●
meyer lemons	○			●
mushrooms, cremini	●	●	●	●
mushrooms, morel	●			
nectarines		●	○	
oranges, navel				●
parsnips	○		●	●
peaches		●	○	
peas, english	●	○		
peas, sugar snap	●	○		
plums		●	○	
pomegranates			●	●
potatoes		●	●	●
potatoes, new	●			
radicchio		●	●	●
rhubarb	●	●		
tangerines	○			●
tomatillos		●	●	
tomatoes		●	○	
truffles			●	
vidalia onions	●			

wines for spring recipes

DISH	PAGE	WINE	NOTES
Sautéed chicken breasts with fava beans and green garlic	17	Crisp white such as Sauvignon Blanc	The "green" flavors in the wine match similar flavors in the recipe
Baked chicken breasts with vidalia onion sauce	18	Soft white such as Viognier	The exotically spiced wine will enhance the natural sweetness of the onions
Lemongrass-chicken soup with baby spring vegetables	22	Soft white such as dry Riesling	Match an aromatic wine with the exotic ingredients in the dish
Parchment-baked chicken with new potatoes, peas, and tarragon	25	Crisp white such as Pinot Gris	A light, crisp wine won't overwhelm the dish's subtle flavors
Pan-roasted chicken with fennel, leeks, and cream	29	Rich white such as White Burgundy	The wine's acid will cut through the richness of the sauce
Stir-fried chicken with sugar snap peas, lemon zest, and mint	30	Crisp white such as Albariño	The crispness of the wine echoes similar flavors in the dish
Baked stuffed chicken breasts with arugula and fontina	33	Pink wine such as dry Rosé	The wine's fruitiness will counter arugula's peppery bite and the cheese's richness
Chicken fricassee with morel mushrooms and thyme	37	Smooth red such as Merlot	The earthiness of the wine is similar to that of the morels
Seared five-spice duck breasts with rhubarb compote	38	Juicy red such as a new-world Pinot Noir	Choose a fruit-forward wine to echo the fruit in the compote
Thai green curry with chicken and asparagus	41	Soft white such as Grüner Veltliner	The acidic wine will provide a nice counterpoint to the dish's spice
Harissa-marinated grilled chicken	44	Juicy red such as Beaujolais	A light, fruity red will stand up to the bold spices in the recipe

wines for summer recipes

DISH	PAGE	WINE	NOTES
Grilled chicken with corn and smoked mozzarella salad	49	Rich white such as a lightly oaked Chardonnay	The wine's oaky nuances will counter the rich cheese and match the corn's nuttiness
Grilled chicken skewers with habanero chile & allspice	50	Soft white such as Gewürztraminer	The sweet, acidic wine will temper the dish's hotness while echoing the warm spices
Grilled chicken with peach-bourbon barbecue sauce	54	Bold red such as a light-bodied Zinfandel	The wine will match the fruitiness of the sauce and counter the chicken's smokiness
Buttermilk-and-herb fried chicken	57	Rich white such as an unoaked Chardonnay	An acidic wine with cut through the fattiness of the dish
Chicken salad with tomatoes, black beans, and cilantro	61	Crisp white such as Pinot Grigio	The wine's acidity will match the tomatoes' while cutting the fattiness of the cheese
Grilled chicken with plum-jalapeño relish	62	Pink wine such as dry Rosé	The wine's fruitiness will match that of the relish while tempering its heat
Grilled butterflied chicken with chimichurri	65	Crisp white such as Albariño	The tart, herbal flavor of the sauce calls for an acidic wine to complement it
Roasted chicken thighs with cherry-thyme compote	69	Juicy red such as a light-bodied Pinot Noir	The dark-meat chicken can stand up to a red, especially one with fruity-herbal hints
Miso-marinated grilled chicken breasts with toasted sesame	70	Rich white such as a lightly oaked Chardonnay	The wine's oak flavor will mimic the nuttiness of both the miso and sesame
Duck tacos with nectarine salsa	73	Pink wine such as dry Rosé	The wine's fruitiness will echo that of the salsa while countering its spiciness
Asian eggplants stuffed with spicy minced chicken	76	Soft white such as Gewürztraminer	An off-dry, aromatic wine will counter the salty-spiciness of the dish

wines for **fall** recipes

DISH	PAGE	WINE	NOTES
Porter-braised chicken thighs with root vegetables	81	Smooth red such as Pinot Noir	A weighty red can stand up to the dark-meat chicken as well as the dish's earthy flavors
Maple-mustard turkey tenderloins with cranberry-port sauce	82	Bold red such as Zinfandel	A big wine with cranberry flavors will complement the bold, fruity sauce
Pomegranate-glazed grilled chicken	86	Pink wine such as a full-bodied dry Rosé	A fruity wine will counter both the smokiness and bitterness of the dish
Bacon-wrapped chicken breasts with warm lentil salad	89	Juicy red such as a light-bodied Pinot Noir	An earthy-fruity wine will match the flavor of the lentils and play off the smoky bacon
Crisp-skin roasted chicken with truffle butter	93	Rich white such as a lightly oaked Chardonnay	The wine's oaky acidity will temper the dish's richness and stand up to the musky truffles
Braised chicken with apples, cider, and brandy	94	Rich white such as White Burgundy	The crisp apple flavors in the wine will echo those in the dish
Roasted chile-spiced chicken with pumpkin seed sauce	97	Juicy red such as Beaujolais	A lightly fruity, earthy, acidic wine will play off the ingredients in the sauce
Cremini-stuffed chicken breasts with porcini pan sauce	98	Smooth red such as Pinot Noir	The wine's earthiness and herbal hints will echo the mushrooms and enhance the dish
Turkey chile verde	102	Crisp white such as Sauvignon Blanc	A wine with racy acidity will match the assertive tartness of the tomatillos
Indian-spiced grilled chicken legs with raita	105	Rich white such as Viognier	The exotic flavors in the wine echo that of the curry powder in the marinade
Cider-brined grill-roasted chicken with grilled apples and sage	109	Soft white such as Riesling	A crisp, apple-scented wine will counter the dish's richness and soften its herbal edge

wines for winter recipes

DISH	PAGE	WINE	NOTES
Smoky roasted chicken breasts with potatoes and sherry sauce	113	Crisp white such as dry Sherry	Use the same sherry as in the recipe for a seamless match
Chicken potpie with root vegetables and thyme crust	114	Rich white such as an unoaked Chardonnay	A weighty wine with good acidity will match a full-bodied dish while cutting its richness
Chicken braised with bacon, onions, and Riesling	118	Soft white such as Riesling	Create a perfect complement by serving the same wine you used in the braising liquid
Sautéed chicken breasts with bitter orange sauce	121	Rich white such as Viognier	A fruity, spice-imbued wine will be a nice complement to the dish
Braised chicken with quick-preserved meyer lemons	125	Crisp white such as Sauvignon Blanc	A pleasantly acidic, herbal wine will stand up to the dish's assertive seasonings
Breaded chicken cutlets with green olive–lemon relish	126	Crisp white such as Pinot Grigio	A lemony wine will match the flavors in the relish and counter the breading's richness
Chicken wings in fermented black bean sauce	129	Soft white such as an off-dry Riesling	A slightly sweet wine will offset the salty, spicy flavors in the dish
Roasted chicken with warm winter greens salad	133	Crisp white such as Sauvignon Blanc	An acidic wine will stand up to the salad dressing and will counter the dish's richness
Claypot caramel chicken with shiitake mushrooms and broccoli	134	Soft white such as an off-dry Gewürztraminer	You'll need a slightly sweet wine to match the caramel flavors in the dish
Mexican lime soup with chicken	137	Crisp white such as Sauvignon Blanc	The wine's tart acidity will match the lime and cut through the rich avocado
Braised chicken with tangerine and star anise	140	Soft white such as Riesling	The wine's citrus flavors and soft sweetness will match the exotic flavors of the dish

glossary

apple cider, hard Apple juice or cider that has been allowed to ferment and develop alcohol is called hard cider.

applejack This brandy made from apples has a deep amber color. Its flavor is slightly sweet, with the distinct flavor of apples.

arugula The leaves of this dark green plant, also called rocket, resemble deeply notched, elongated oak leaves. They have a nutty, tangy, and slightly peppery flavor. Mature arugula is often more pungent than mild, tender baby arugula.

avocado Rich in flavor and silky in texture, avocados are a favorite subtropical fruit. Almost-black Hass avocados are especially prized for their buttery flesh.

baking powder A leavening agent for baked goods and sometimes fried foods, baking powder consists of baking soda, an acid, and a stabilizer. Liquid, and, in the case of double-acting baking powder, heat, activates the baking powder, releasing carbon dioxide gas, thereby causing batters to rise.

bourbon An American-made whiskey with a corn base, bourbon is aged in charred oak barrels, which gives the spirit its deep golden amber color and smoky flavor.

brandy This spirit is distilled from wine or fermented fruit juice that has been aged in wood, which adds both color and flavor.

buttermilk In earlier times, buttermilk was the milky liquid that remained after cream was churned into butter. Today, it is made by adding a bacterial culture to milk, giving it a tangy flavor and thick texture.

Calvados This oak-aged apple brandy comes from Normandy, France, where it is sipped as a digestif as well as used in both sweet and savory dishes.

capers Flower buds from a shrub native to the Mediterranean, capers are usually sold pickled in a vinegar brine. Those labeled "nonpareils," from the south of France, are the smallest and considered the best.

cayenne pepper A very hot red pepper made from ground dried cayenne chiles, cayenne is used sparingly to add heat or to heighten flavor.

celery root Also known as celeriac, celery root is a knobby, round fall and winter vegetable that contributes a subtle celery flavor when cooked and a crisp crunch to salads when used raw.

cheese Cheese adds unique flavor and texture to many recipes. Visit a specialty cheese shop with a rapid turnover for the freshest and best-quality cheeses.

fontina A rich, semifirm cow's milk cheese with an earthy, mild flavor, Italian fontina val d'Aosta hails from Italy's Piedmont region. Non-Italian versions of the cheese are lacking in flavor, but all are excellent for melting.

mozzarella, smoked Smoked mozzarella, sometimes called *mozzarella affumicata*, is fresh mozzarella that has been smoked, which gives it a dark exterior color, a slightly dry, firm texture, and a smoky flavor.

queso fresco This fresh Mexican cheese has a salty, mild flavor and a dry, crumbly texture.

ricotta salata A variation on ricotta cheese, ricotta salata has a firm, dry texture and a salty, mild, and slightly milky flavor.

chiles When buying fresh chiles, seek out plump, firm, unblemished specimens. Use caution when handling chiles, as their heat is easily transferred to the skin; wearing a rubber glove is a good precautionary measure.

Anaheim Anaheim chiles are 6 to 10 inches in length and are bright green in color. They have a very mild heat and vegetal flavor.

habanero This small, lantern-shaped chile comes in red, orange, and green colors. It is often considered the hottest of the chiles, but in addition to a fiery, intense heat, they boast a fruity, citrusy flavor.

jalapeño This bright green chile, averaging about 2 inches in length, ranges from hot to very hot and is one of the the most widely used chiles in the United States.

serrano Serrano chiles are slightly smaller in size than jalapeños, but typically have a little more heat. They are often sold in their green state, although red serrano chiles are sometimes available.

Thai Tiny tiny chiles are red or green in color and measure about 1 inch in length. They are very seedy and have a searing heat.

coconut milk, unsweetened Sold in cans, coconut milk is made by processing grated coconut and water. The thick fat, or coconut cream, rises to the top of the liquid. For curries, this cream is often spooned off and used to fry the curry paste.

crème fraîche In the French tradition, crème fraîche is unpasteurized cream thickened by bacteria that is naturally present in the cream. More commonly, though, it is cream thickened by a bacteria that is added, yielding a soft, spreadable consistency and a tangy, slightly nutty flavor.

crystallized ginger Sometimes called candied ginger, crystallized ginger is made by cooking ginger in a sugar syrup and then coating it with coarse sugar crystals. It is usually sold in thin slices.

curry paste, Thai green This flavor base for spicy Thai green curry is made from a mixture of fresh green chiles, garlic, cilantro, lemongrass, shallots, shrimp paste, and other seasonings and spices. It is sold in small jars in well-stocked grocery stores and in Southeast Asian markets.

curry powder Curry powder is a convenience product meant to simplify the daily chore of blending spices for Indian cooks. It is a complex mixture of ground chiles, spices, seeds, and herbs.

fermented black beans This Chinese ingredient is made by preserving black soybeans in salt. Before use, the beans must be rinsed of excess salt; they are also sometimes soaked in water to reduce their saltiness. Fermented black beans are often sold packed in plastic bags; look for them in Asian markets.

fish sauce, Asian Made from salted and fermented fish, fish sauce is a thin, clear liquid that ranges in color from amber to dark brown. Southeast Asians use it in the same way Westerners use salt, both as a cooking ingredient and as a seasoning at the table.

five-spice powder, Chinese This aromatic blend of five spices includes cinnamon, cloves, star anise, Sichuan peppercorns, and fennel or anise seeds. In some versions, ground ginger takes the place of one of the other spices.

green garlic Immature garlic shoots, green garlic stalks resemble green onions, but they taste of garlic, without garlic's pungency. They are available only in the spring.

harissa This fiery North African spice paste is used both as a seasoning and as a condiment. It is made with chiles, spices, garlic, and olive oil and is sold in tubes, cans, or jars in well-stocked grocery stores and some Middle Eastern markets.

hickory chips Hickory, a hardwood, is made into wood chips that, when soaked in water and added to a hot grill, create a fragrant, woodsy smoke to flavor all types of foods.

hoisin sauce A thick, brown, salty-sweet sauce, hoisin sauce is used both as an ingredient and as a condiment in Chinese cooking. It is made with soybeans, garlic, vinegar, chiles, and other flavorful spices.

lemongrass This herb with a fresh lemon flavor, but with none of lemon's brassiness, resembles a green onion with pale gray-green leaves. The tender inner core contains the most flavor. Lemongrass is a common flavoring in Southeast Asian cooking.

maple syrup, pure Maple syrup is made by boiling down the sap of the sugar maple tree to an amber-colored syrup. The syrup is graded according to color. Cooking maple

and grade B are the darkest in color and have robust flavor; grade A syrup has a lighter color and flavor.

Meyer lemon Believed to be a cross between a regular lemon and a mandarin orange, Meyer lemons are thin skinned and turn deep orangish yellow when ripe. Their fragrant juice and flesh are sweeter and less acidic than regular lemons.

mirin An important ingredient in Japanese cooking, mirin is a sweet cooking wine made by fermenting glutinous rice and sugar. The pale gold and syrupy wine adds a rich flavor and translucent sheen to sauces, dressings, and simmered dishes.

miso, white A staple of the Japanese kitchen, miso is a fermented paste of soybeans and grain. Relatively mild-tasting white miso, or shiro-miso, is one of the more common varieties. Look for miso in the refrigerator case of well-stocked grocery or natural foods stores, or in Japanese markets.

mushrooms A wide array of mushroom varieties is available to cooks these days. Each type has a unique flavor and texture.

cremini Resembling white button mushrooms in shape and size, cremini are mottled brown in color. They have a firmer texture and fuller flavor than white mushrooms.

morel The morel has an intense, musky flavor for which it is highly prized. This uncultivated mushroom has a dark, elongated, sponge-like cap and hollow stem. Unlike other mushrooms, morels should be immersed briefly in a large bowl of water to dislodge the sand that tends to fill their crevices.

porcini, dried Dried porcini mushrooms are sold in well-stocked grocery stores and specialty markets. They have an intensely savory aroma and flavor. When cooking with them, just a small amount adds a full, woodsy flavor. When buying, look for packages with large pieces and very few small, crumbly bits.

shiitake, dried Originally from Japan, shiitake mushrooms are now widely available in the U.S. Dried shiitakes have a very earthy, meaty aroma and flavor. Look for those with pale cracks in the caps' surfaces.

oils There is a wide variety of oils available to cooks today. Some are best used for high-heat cooking, some for drizzling over a finished dish as a flavor accent.

canola This neutral-tasting oil is pressed from rapeseed, a relative of the mustard plant. High in monounsaturated fat, it is good for general cooking. It also has a high smoking point and can be used for frying.

extra-virgin olive The first cold pressing of olives yields extra-virgin olive oil, the variety

that is the lowest in acid and the purest, with a full flavor that reflects where the olives were grown.

grape seed This oil from the crushed seeds of grapes has a high smoking point and a mild flavor; it is high in healthful monounsaturated fat.

peanut Oil made from peanuts can be heated to quite a high temperature before it begins to smoke, so it is good for stir-frying and deep-frying. It has a faintly nutty flavor.

sesame, Asian This deep amber–colored oil is pressed from toasted sesame seeds. It has a strong flavor and should be used sparingly as a seasoning in Asian-inspired dishes.

panko These Japanese bread crumbs have a coarse, but very light and airy, texture. Look for panko in well-stocked grocery stores and Asian markets.

paprika, smoked sweet A Spanish specialty, smoked paprika is made from red chiles that have been smoked and then ground. It has a very earthy, smoky, and almost meaty flavor and a deep red color. Smoked paprika is available in sweet or mild (dulce), bittersweet (agridulce), and hot (picante) varieties.

pumpkin seeds, shelled Also called pepitas, shelled pumpkin seeds are green in color and have a slightly sweet, nutty flavor.

Port, tawny or ruby True Port, a sweet fortified wine with jammy, concentrated flavors, hails from Portugal. There a few different varieties of Port, but for cooking, look for a reasonably priced ruby or tawny Port, rather than an expensive vintage Port.

porter This dark beer is made with roasted malt. It has a robust, slightly smoky flavor and an assertive bitterness.

rice wine, Chinese Also known as Shaoxing wine, Chinese rice wine is made from glutinous rice and is used for both cooking and sipping. Look for it in Asian grocery stores.

sake Referred to as a "wine," this Japanese beverage is made not from grapes, but from fermented rice. Colorless or very pale, sake comes in several varieties and is often used in cooking.

sherry, dry A fortified wine originating in Southern Spain, sherry is made from the Palomino Fino grape. Dry sherry is mild in sweetness and is often used in cooking.

Sriracha sauce This bright red-orange sauce is a mixture of ground chiles, tomatoes, vinegar, garlic, salt, and sugar. Originating in southern Thailand, the general-purpose sauce is used sparingly to add zest to a wide range of cooked dishes. It is also used as a table condiment for many Southeast Asian foods. Look for it in well-stocked grocery stores and Asian markets.

star anise These deep brown, star-shaped pods have a flavor much like that of their namesake, aniseed, but with a more savory and assertive quality. They are native to China and, ground into powder, are a component in Chinese five-spice powder.

tomatillos Tomatillos resemble small, firm green tomatoes enclosed in a papery husk. Their flavor is faintly fruity and tart, with a slight vegetal quality. Before use, peel off and discard the husks and rinse the tomatillos to wash away the sticky residue on the skins. Look for tomatillos in the produce section of well-stocked grocery stores or Latin-American markets.

truffles, black or white Truffles, round, wrinkly, and highly prized underground fungi, traditionally grow under oak trees in France and Italy, and are sniffed out by dogs or pigs during the fall season. The Périgord area of France is known for its black truffles and Piedmont region of Italy for its white truffles. The fragrance and flavor of truffles is exceptionally rich and earthy. Their intensity requires that only very little be used to season foods.

vermouth This fortified wine is infused with herbs and spices. It available in sweet (red) and dry (white) varieties. Dry white vermouth is an ingredient in a classic martini and is often used in cooking.

vinegars Each type of vinegar has a unique flavor profile and acidity that makes it particularly suited to certain dishes.

balsamic A specialty of the Italian region of Emilia-Romagna, balsamic vinegar is an aged vinegar made from the unfermented grape juice, or must, of Trebbiano grapes. Aged in a series of wooden casks of decreasing sizes, each of a different wood, balsamic grows sweeter and more mellow with time.

balsamic, white This nontraditional version of balsamic vinegar has the sweet-tart flavor of regular balsamic vinegar, but a light color that will not darken the foods to which it is added.

cider Made from apples, cider vinegar is noted for its distinctive apple flavor. For the best results, buy real apple cider vinegar, not cider-flavored distilled vinegar.

red wine Sharply acidic, red wine vinegar is produced when red wine is fermented for a second time.

sherry True sherry vinegar from Spain, labeled "vinagre de Jerez," has a slightly sweet, nutty taste, a result of aging in oak.

index

OXMOOR HOUSE

Oxmoor House books are distributed by Sunset Books
80 Willow Road, Menlo Park, CA 94025
Telephone: 650 324 1532
VP and Associate Publisher Jim Childs
Director of Marketing Sydney Webber
Oxmoor House and Sunset Books are divisions
of Southern Progress Corporation

WILLIAMS-SONOMA, INC.
Founder & Vice-Chairman Chuck Williams

WILLIAMS-SONOMA NEW FLAVORS SERIES
Conceived and produced by Weldon Owen Inc.
415 Jackson Street, Suite 200, San Francisco, CA 94111
Telephone: 415 291 0100 Fax: 415 291 8841
www.weldonowen.com

In Collaboration with Williams-Sonoma, Inc.
3250 Van Ness Avenue, San Francisco, CA 94109

A WELDON OWEN PRODUCTION

First printed in 2008
Printed in Singapore

10 9 8 7 6 5 4 3 2 1
Library of Congress Cataloging-in-Publication Data is available.

ISBN-13: 978-0-8487-3254-7
ISBN-10: 0-8487-3254-5

This book is printed with paper harvested from well-managed forests
utilizing sustainable and environmentally sound practices.

WELDON OWEN INC.

Executive Chairman, Weldon Owen Group John Owen
CEO and President, Weldon Owen Inc. Terry Newell
Senior VP, International Sales Stuart Laurence
VP, Sales and New Business Development Amy Kaneko
Director of Finance Mark Perrigo

VP and Publisher Hannah Rahill
Executive Editor Jennifer Newens
Senior Editor Dawn Yanagihara
Associate Editor Julia Humes

VP and Creative Director Gaye Allen
Art Director Kara Church
Senior Designer Ashley Martinez
Designer Stephanie Tang
Photo Manager Meghan Hildebrand

Production Director Chris Hemesath
Production Manager Michelle Duggan
Color Manager Teri Bell

Photographers Tucker + Hossler
Food Stylist Alison Attenborough
Prop Stylist Lauren Hunter

Additional Photography Kate Sears: page 105; Fotosearch: Photodisk, pages
14–15; Age Fotostock, page 52; Veer: Staffan Anderson, page 26; Getty Images:
Oswald Eckstein, page 35, Barry Wong, page 101; Corbis: Roy Morsch, pages
46–47; Jupiter Images: Evan Skiar, pages 78–79; Shutterstock: Inacio Pires,
pages 110–111

ACKNOWLEDGMENTS

Weldon Owen wishes to thank the following individuals for their kind
assistance: Food Stylist Assistant Lillian Kang; Copy editor Sharon Silva;
Proofreaders Kathryn Shedrick and Lesli Neilson; Indexer Ken DellaPenta